Second Edition
STUDENT WORKBOOK
for
PROGRAMMING OF
CNC MACHINES

By

Ken Evans

Industrial Press Inc.
New York

First Edition, May 2007
Sponsoring Editor: John Carleo
Cover and text Design: Janet Romano

INDUSTRIAL PRESS INC.

989 Avenue of the Americas, New York, NY 10018

PROGRAMMING OF
CNC MACHINES
STUDENT WORKBOOK

Second Edition

Notice to the reader: While every possible effort has been made to insure the accuracy of the information presented herein, the authors and publisher express no guarantee of the same. The authors and publisher do not offer any warrant or guarantee that omissions or errors have not occurred and may not be held liable for any damages resulting from the use of this text by the readers. The readers accept the full responsibility for their own safety and that of the equipment used in connection with the instructions in this text. There has been no attempt to cover all controllers or machine types used in the industry and the reader should consult the operation and programming manuals of the machines they are using before any operation or programming is attempted.

Printed in the United States

2   3   4   5   6   7   8   9   10

ACKNOWLEDGEMENTS

I give thanks first, to God, for blessing me with the opportunity, knowledge and ability to share in this work. Many thanks are due to all: my Publisher, Industrial Press, Inc., President, Alex Luchars; Marketing Director/Editor, John Carleo; Production Manager, Janet Romano; and Product Manager, Suzanne Remore; Richard Jones of Technical Training Systems/Lab Technologies for AutoCad software; Sandvik Coromant for tooling drawings and other technical data; Greg Mercurio, of Shop Floor Automations for allowing the use of Predator Virtual CNC V7.0 software for verification of the programs and, CarrLane Manufacturing for technical data charts.

PREFACE

There are many textbooks written on the subject of CNC Programming that include a multitude of practical examples; however, very few include enough practice exercises for the learner to verify their understanding. This edition of "Programming of CNC Machines Student Workbook" provides many practical exercises designed to verify comprehension of CNC programming. While this workbook is written as a companion to "Programming of CNC Machines", Third Edition, it may be used by anyone (no matter where they have learned about CNC programming) to confirm his or her knowledge of CNC programming. Although there are many ways to program a part in order to get the accurate results, one proven method is offered in the answer key that is consistent with the companion text. Most important, is that the part is made to specifications, safely and efficiently. While it is possible for someone to program a CNC machine without much machining experience, the result will be better if a practical background exists. Feeds & speeds, tool selection and work holding methods are very hard to learn from a book and it is proven that practical experience is the best teacher. It is also a plus to have a thorough understanding of shop mathematics. A student who has been taught the basic fundamentals in these maters, beforehand, will have the most success writing CNC programs in the long term.

This workbook should be used to verify that you have learned the basic skills necessary to write a CNC program, line-by-line, to make a variety of workpieces. An answer key is provided at the end of this book to verify correct programming. Try to complete as many questions and examples as possible, without using the answer key. It would be better to use the text (Programming of CNC Machines, Third Edition) to look up the required information, rather than go to the answers. The text is a reference tool, just like your machinist tools, it was designed to help you get the job done. Whenever it is possible, consult with your trainer for additional ideas or methods to evaluate your work.

TABLE OF CONTENTS

CNC BASICS

Process Planning

Anytime a new part is considered for manufacture, it is necessary to have a logical plan in order to machine it efficiently. The following is an explanation of the exercise requirement: There are three Process Planning Sheets on the following pages (copy as many as needed) and CNC Programming Sheets are included for each section of Turning and Machining Center Programming. Please refer to the book "Programming of CNC Machines" Third Edition, Part 1, CNC Basics, for a detailed description of the use of these documents. You may also find a list of cutting tools that can be used for preparation of the Process Planning Sheets in each respective Turning and Machining Center section of this workbook.

Use the Operation Sheet to identify each individual operation and the machines necessary to complete the part in the following blueprints.

Use the CNC Setup Sheet to identify work holding, cutting tools, work piece coordinate zero locations and any other pertinent information needed to complete the part setup for the following blueprints. Refer to the tool list provided in the Turning and Machining Center sections of this workbook to choose the appropriate tools.

Use the Quality Control Check Sheet to list 100% of the dimensional data needed to verify that the parts are made to specification in the following blueprints.

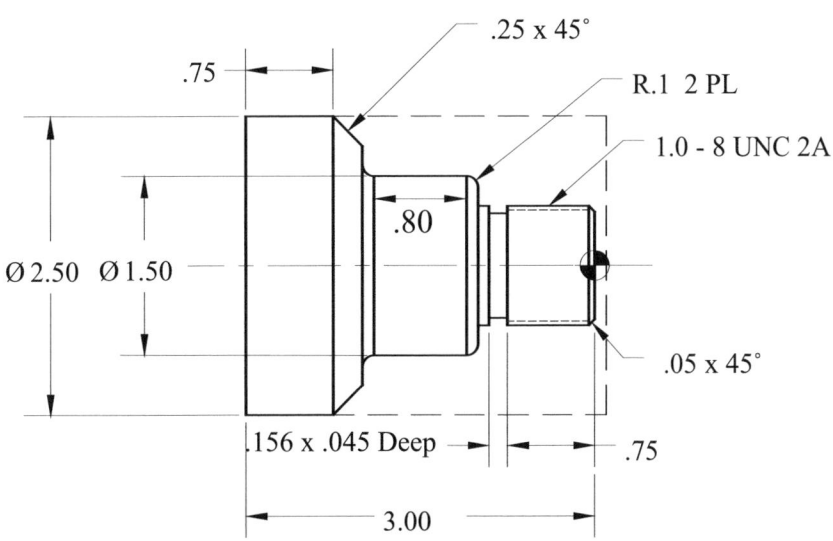

Figure 1   Turning Center Process Planning

1

Chart 1
Process Planning Operation Sheet

Date:		Prepared By:	
Part Name:		Part Number:	
Quantity:		Sheet ___ of ___	
Material:			
Raw Stock Size:			
Operation Number	Machine Used	Description of Operation	Time

In this example, the parts are provided as 3.0625 long slugs with one end having been already faced. It will be necessary to clamp the 2.50 diameter in pre-machined soft jaws with enough material extended to allow machining of the part including removal of 1/16 inch from the face of the part. The material is 4340 alloy steel. Dimensional tolerances are as follows: .X = plus or minus .015 inch, .XX = plus or minus .010 inch, .XXX = plus or minus .005 inch and angular tolerance is plus or minus 1/2°. Please use the copies of the Process Planning sheets and develop a plan to machine the part to dimensional requirements.

Chart 2
Process Planning CNC Setup Sheet

Date:	Prepared By:
Part Name:	Part Number:
Machine:	Program Number:

Workpiece Zero: X _____ Y _____ Z _____

Setup Description:

Tool #	Tool Description	Offset #	Comments

Chart 3
Process Planning
Quality Control Check Sheet

Date:			Checked By:
Part Name:		Part Number:	

Blueprint Dimension	Tolerance	Actual Dimension	Comments

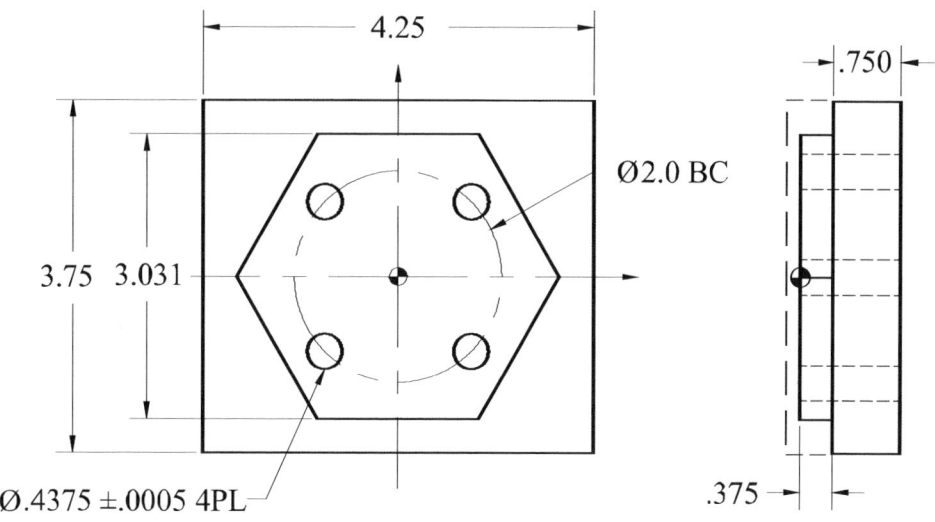

Figure 2   Machining Center Process Planning

In this example, it will be necessary to machine the part from a solid blank of Aluminum that is pre-machined to 4.25 square and is 1.25 thick. The top surface must have .125 inch of material removed, as well. Dimensional tolerances are as follows: .X = plus or minus .015 inch, .XX = plus or minus .010 inch, .XXX = plus or minus .005 inch and angular tolerance is plus or minus 1/2°. Please use the copies of the Process Planning sheets and develop a plan to machine the part to dimensional requirements. Make your tool selections from the CNC Machining Center Tool List in the CNC Machining Center Programming section of this workbook.

CNC Student Workbook

Chart 1
Process Planning Operation Sheet

Date:		Prepared By:	
Part Name:		Part Number:	
Quantity:		Sheet ___ of ___	
Material:			
Raw Stock Size:			

Operation Number	Machine Used	Description of Operation	Time

Chart 2
Process Planning CNC Setup Sheet

Date:	Prepared By:
Part Name:	Part Number:
Machine:	Program Number:

Workpiece Zero: X _____ Y _____ Z _____

Setup Description:

Tool #	Tool Description	Offset #	Comments

Chart 3
Process Planning
Quality Control Check Sheet

Date:			Checked By:
Part Name:		Part Number:	

Blueprint Dimension	Tolerance	Actual Dimension	Comments

Feeds and Speeds

The following charts are supplied for use in answering the exercise problems presented here. The Surface Feet per Minute (SFPM) and Feed in inches per revolution (in/rev) values represented here are given in ranges. The user should note that the values starting at the low end of the range are intended as a minimum starting point for calculations, and at the high end, as a maximum recommended SFPM and Feed. Final values used for machining may differ based on many factors. As you answer the problems, use values that are within the ranges given. Refer to the text "Programming of CNC Machines" Part 1 CNC Basics, Metal Cutting Factors for detailed information regarding Feed and Speed calculations. Also note, a more comprehensive source for machining data is the *Machinery's Handbook* and that other valuable sources for machining data are in the tool and insert catalogs supplied by cutting tool manufacturers.

Feeds and Speeds Chart for Turning

	Tool Material	
Material	**High Speed Steel**	**Carbide**
Carbon Steel SFPM Feed in/rev	30 - 160 .006 - .012	200 - 1300 .008 - .036
Alloy Steel SFPM Feed in/rev	30 - 120 .006 - .012	125 - 1000 .008 - .036
Stainless Steel SFPM Feed in/rev	25 - 110 .006 - .012	80 - 945 .007 - .036
Aluminum SFPM Feed in/rev	500 - 800 .006 - .012	2800 - 4500 .017 - .036

Note: *As a general rule, the minimum depth of cut should be 1.5 to 2 times the tool nose radius and the maximum feed rate should be approximately one half the tool nose radius for rough turning using carbide inserts.*

For milling, the maximum depth of cut is equal to the flute length or the insert height and the maximum width of cut is the cutter diameter. However, this is not practical in most cases. A more widely used practice is to set the maximum depth of cut to 2/3 of the flute length and the maximum width of cut to 2/3 of the diameter, as well. These basic conditions should be followed for the remainder of this workbook. Drilling calculations should be based on High Speed Steel (HSS) values for Turning and HSS End Mill values for Milling.

Feeds and Speeds Chart for Milling

	HSS End Mill	Carbide End Mill	Carbide Inserted Face Mill
Carbon Steel **SFPM** **Feed in/tooth**	25 - 140 .001 - .004	210 - 1000 .006 - .012	90 - 685 .020 - .039
Alloy Steel **SFPM** **Feed in/tooth**	5 - 85 .001 - .004	40 - 450 .006 - .012	39 - 475 .020 - .039
Stainless Steel **SFPM** **Feed in/tooth**	20 - 80 .001 - .003	200 - 700 .006 - .012	210 - 385 .020 - .039
Aluminum **SFPM** **Feed in/tooth**	165 - 850 .002 - .006	600 - 2000 .008 - .015	755 - 1720 .020 - .039

Refer to the following formula needed to calculate revolutions per minute (r/min).

$$r/\min = \frac{12 \times CS}{\pi \times D}$$

Where

CS = Cutting Speed from the range in the charts above or the *Machinery's Handbook*

π = 3.1417

D = Diameter of the workpiece or the cutter.

Refer to the charts above or the *Machinery's Handbook* for the feed in inches per tooth, (in/tooth) for chip load recommendations and review the formula below that is necessary to calculate the feed aspect of the metal-cutting operation.

$$F = R \times N \times f$$

Where

F = Feed rate in inches per minute (in/min)

R = r/min calculated from the preceding formula

N = the number of cutting edges

f = the chip load, per tooth, recommended from the charts above or the *Machinery's Handbook*.

1. On a CNC lathe, a facing cut is needed to establish the part-zero surface. The Alloy Steel bar stock is 2.5 inches in diameter and has 1/32 inch of excess material to be removed from each side. A carbide-inserted tool with a 1/32 inch nose radius will be used for this operation. Since the diameter changes as the tool travels toward the centerline, what would the r/min be? What would the SFPM be? What would the depth of cut be?

2. When finish turning an aluminum bar that is 2.3125 inch in diameter with a carbide-inserted turning tool that has a 1/64 inch tool nose radius, what is the r/min and feed rate required if the depth of cut is 1/64 inch per side?

3. An internal threading operation is required on a CNC lathe to make a 1-8 UNC thread in a Carbon Steel part. The cutting tool material is High Speed Steel. What would the r/min be for this operation?

4. Calculate the appropriate speeds and feeds for each of the required tools in the lathe process planning project above and enter your answers on your CNC Setup sheet in the comments section.

5. Calculate the appropriate speeds and feeds for each of the required tools in the mill process planning project above and enter your answers on your CNC Setup sheet in the comments section.

6. In this example, the material is Stainless Steel. A .5625 inch diameter hole is to be drilled through a plate that is 1.25 inch thick. Calculate the r/min and feed rate best suited for this operation. Use the HSS End Mill values from the chart.

7. A Carbon Steel plate 4.0 inches square requires a 2.0 inch diameter hole to be machined through the center. A pre-drilling operation uses a 1.25 inch diameter HSS drill and a finishing operation uses a .875 diameter 4-fluted HSS end mill to circle mill out the remainder of material. What is the r/min and feed rate for the drill? What is the r/min and feed rate for the end mill?

8. A 5-tooth 3.0 inch diameter carbide face mill is used to machine an Alloy Steel bar that is 2.0 inches wide and 6.0 inches long. There are two depth passes of .080 inch each required to bring the part to size. What is the r/min and feed rate for this cut?

9. A 4.0 inch flat aluminum bar requires a profile to be cut on both ends. A 2-fluted HSS end mill 7/16 inch in diameter has been selected for the job. The part thickness is .5 inch and the amount of axial metal removal is .25 inch. What is the appropriate r/min and feed rate?

10. Use the formula and data given above to calculate the feed and speed required for each tool in the programming exercises that follow and list your results in the comments section of the CNC Setup Sheet.

Coordinate Systems

1. Use the following drawing (Figure 3) to identify the absolute coordinates for each axis and for each point of the profile of the turned part, based on diametrical considerations.

2. Use the following drawing (Figure 3) to identify the incremental coordinates for each axis and for each point of the profile of the turned part, based on radial considerations.

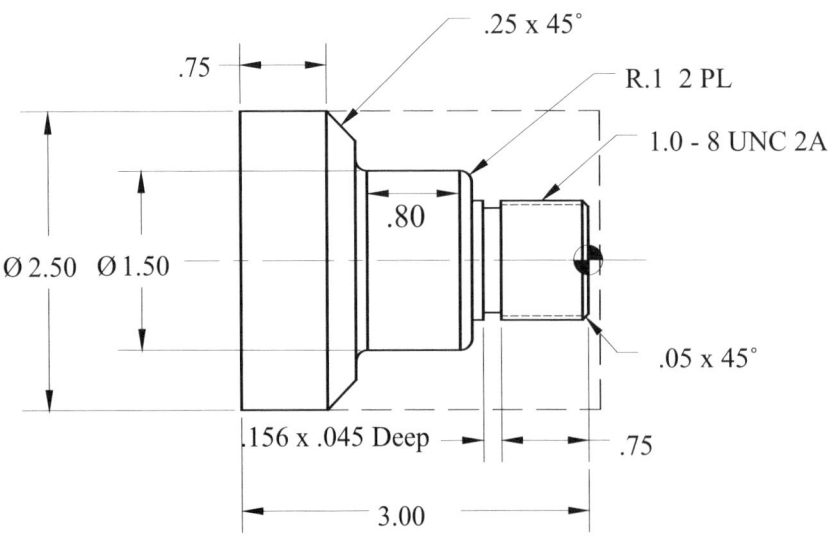

Figure 3   Identify Absolute and Incremental Coordinates

3. Use the following drawing (Figure 4) to identify the absolute coordinates for each axis and for each point of the profile of the milled part. Start at part zero and proceed clockwise.

4. Use the following drawing (Figure 4) to identify the incremental coordinates for each axis and for each point of the profile of the milled part.

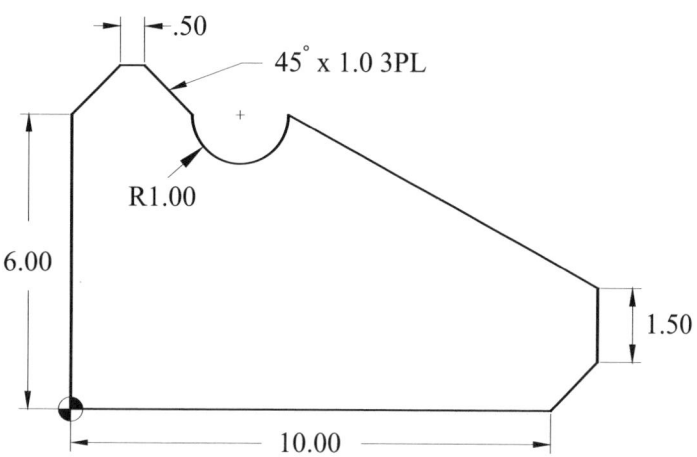

Figure 4   Identify Absolute and Incremental Coordinates

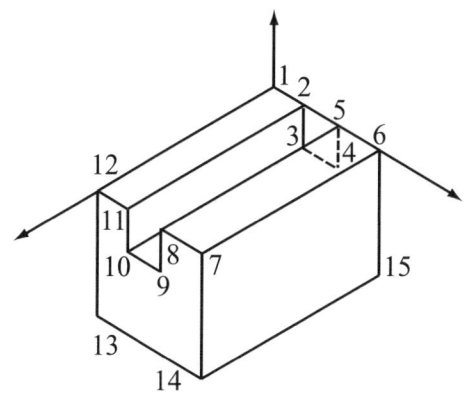

Figure 5   Identify Absolute Coordinates

5. List the absolute coordinate values for X, Y and Z for each of the 15 points as indicated on the drawing (Figure 5). The part is 3.0 inches long, 2.0 inches wide and has a height of 2.25 inches. The slot is cut through the centerline of the width and is .50 wide and .375 deep.

6. Identify each axis (vertical milling representation) and its positive or negative value on the drawing (Figure 6).

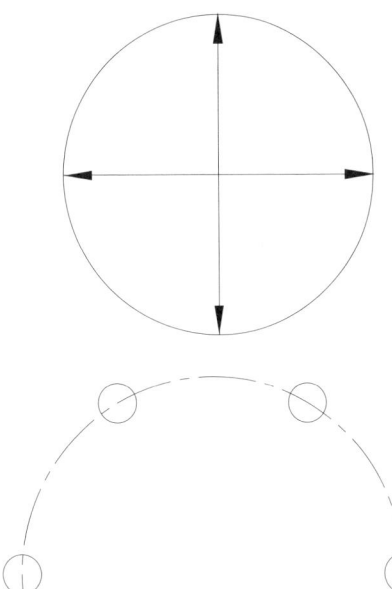

**Figure 6   Identify Vertical Milling Axes, Polar
Rotation, Quadrants and Angular Values**

Ø5.0 BC

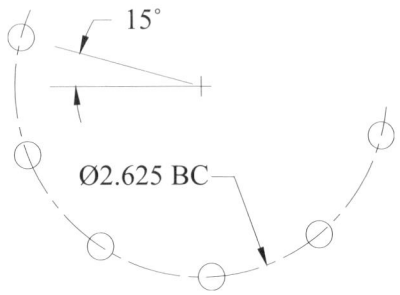

Figure 7
Identify Polar Coordinate Values

Figure 8
Identify Polar Coordinate Values

7. Indicate the negative rotation direction for the polar coordinate system on the drawing (Figure 6).

8. Indicate each of the polar quadrants on the drawing (Figure 6).

9. Identify the angular value locations for 0, 90, 180, and 270 degrees on the drawing (Figure 6).

10. Identify the polar (angular and radial) values for each of the holes on the drawing (Figure 7).

11. Identify the polar (angular and radial) values for each of the holes on the drawing (Figure 8).

Trigonometric Calculations

In many cases, it will be necessary to calculate the coordinate values of points for input into your CNC programs. The exercises that follow are a small sampling of the types of problems you are likely to encounter. Use your calculation skills to answer all of the problems and to prepare yourself for others, when you complete the actual programming exercises in the CNC Turning and Machining Center sections of this workbook.

The following two charts are provided for your benefit. Many of the formulas shown are needed to complete the problems.

1. In order to program the following part, it will be necessary to identify the absolute rectangular coordinate location for the center point for each hole. List the coordinate values for each, starting with the hole at the one O'clock position and proceeding clockwise. The angular value for this hole is 70 degrees.

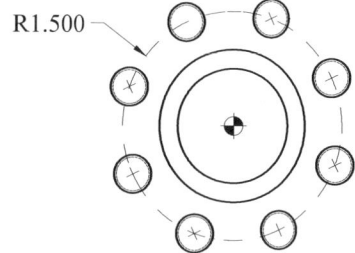

Figure 9   Calculate Absolute Coordinates

2. In order to inspect the part in the following drawing (Figure 10) to specification, a center-to-center dimension is required. Use the data given to calculate what this dimension would be.

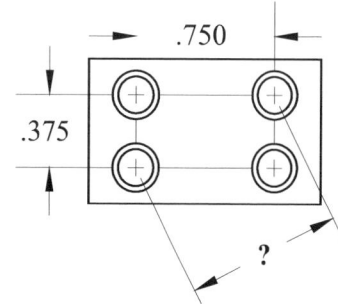

Figure 10   Calculate the Center to Center Distance

3. Use the following drawing (Figure 11) to calculate the values for the unknown distance.

4. Use the following drawing (Figure 12) to calculate the values for each chord distance.

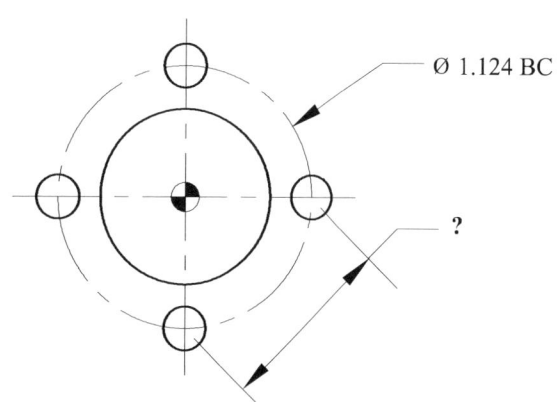

Figure 11 Calculate the Center to Center Distance

RIGHT TRIANGLES

Known Sides and Angles	Unknown Sides and Angles			Area
a and b	$c = \sqrt{a^2 + b^2}$	$A = \arctan\dfrac{a}{b}$	$B = \arctan\dfrac{b}{a}$	$\dfrac{a \times b}{2}$
a and c	$b = \sqrt{c^2 - a^2}$	$A = \arcsin\dfrac{a}{c}$	$A = \arccos\dfrac{a}{c}$	$\dfrac{a \times \sqrt{c^2 - a^2}}{2}$
b and c	$a = \sqrt{c^2 - b^2}$	$A = \arccos\dfrac{b}{c}$	$B = \arcsin\dfrac{b}{c}$	$\dfrac{b \times \sqrt{c^2 - b^2}}{2}$
a and $\angle\,A$	$b = \dfrac{a}{\tan A}$	$c = \dfrac{a}{\sin A}$	$B = 90° - A$	$\dfrac{a^2}{2 \times \tan A}$
a and $\angle\,B$	$b = a \times \tan B$	$c = \dfrac{a}{\cos B}$	$A = 90° - B$	$\dfrac{a^2 \times \tan B}{2}$
b and $\angle\,A$	$a = b \times \tan A$	$c = \dfrac{b}{\cos A}$	$B = 90° - A$	$\dfrac{b^2 \times \tan A}{2}$
b and $\angle\,B$	$a = \dfrac{b}{\tan B}$	$c = \dfrac{b}{\sin B}$	$A = 90° - B$	$\dfrac{b^2}{2 \times \tan B}$
c and $\angle\,A$	$a = c \times \sin A$	$b = c \times \cos A$	$B = 90° - A$	$c^2 \times \sin A \times \cos$
c and $\angle\,B$	$a = c \times \cos B$	$b = c \times \sin B$	$A = 90° - B$	$c^2 \times \sin B \times \cos$

The triangle diagram (in the header row): right triangle with vertices labeled A, B, $C = 90°$; side a opposite A, side b opposite B, side c opposite C (the hypotenuse).

OBLIQUE TRIANGLES

Known Sides and Angles	Unknown Sides and Angles			Area
All three sides a, b, c	$A=$ $\arccos \dfrac{b^2+c^2-a^2}{2bc}$	$B=$ $\arcsin \dfrac{b \times \sin A}{a}$	$C=$ $180° - A - B$	$\dfrac{a \times b \times \sin C}{2}$
Two sides and the angle between them a, b, $\angle C$	$c=$ $\sqrt{a^2+b^2-\left(2ab \times \cos C\right)}$	$A=$ $\arctan \dfrac{a \times \sin C}{b-\left(a \times \cos C\right)}$	$B=$ $180° - A - C$	$\dfrac{a \times b \times \sin C}{2}$
Two sides and the angle opposite one of the sides a, b, $\angle A$ ($\angle B$ less than $90°$)	$B=$ $\arcsin \dfrac{b \times \sin A}{a}$	$C=$ $180° - A - B$	$c=$ $\dfrac{a \times \sin C}{\sin A}$	$\dfrac{a \times b \times \sin C}{2}$
Two sides and the angle opposite one of the sides a, b, $\angle A$ ($\angle B$ greater than $90°$)	$B=$ $180° -$ $\arcsin \dfrac{b \times \sin A}{a}$	$C=$ $180° - A - B$	$c=$ $\dfrac{a \times \sin C}{\sin A}$	$\dfrac{a \times b \times \sin C}{2}$
One side and two angles a, $\angle A$, $\angle B$	$b=$ $\dfrac{a \times \sin B}{\sin A}$	$C=$ $180° - A - B$	$c=$ $\dfrac{a \times \sin C}{\sin A}$	$\dfrac{a \times b \times \sin C}{2}$

5. Calculate the amount of tool travel necessary, to allow for the drill point, to drill through a .562 inch thick plate using the following drill Diameter with a standard drill point angle of 118° degrees (Figure 13).

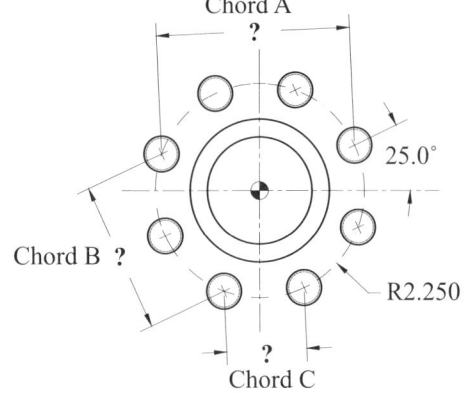

Figure 12 Calculate Chord Distances

6. Calculate the depth of cut required using a #5 (Plain Type) center drill to countersink to a diameter of .395 inch. Plain Type center drills have an angle of 60° with a point angle of 120°. The length from the end of the point angle to the beginning of the 60° angle is 3/16 inch (See *Machinery's Handbook*) (Figure 14).

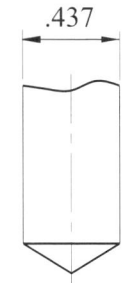

Figure 13
Calculate for Drill Point
Compensation

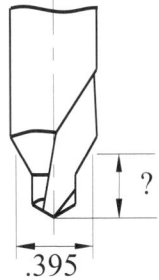

Figure 14
Calculate for Drill Point
Compensation

7. Calculate the amount of tool travel necessary, to allow for the drill point plus .090, to drill through a .875 thick plate using the following drill diameter and with a drill point angle of 135 degrees (Figure 15).

8. The profile of a part is to be machined using a .500 inch diameter end mill as shown Figure 16. Calculate the necessary offset amount for each axis and the coordinate values that will be required for the CNC program.

Figure 15
Calculate for Drill Point
Compensation

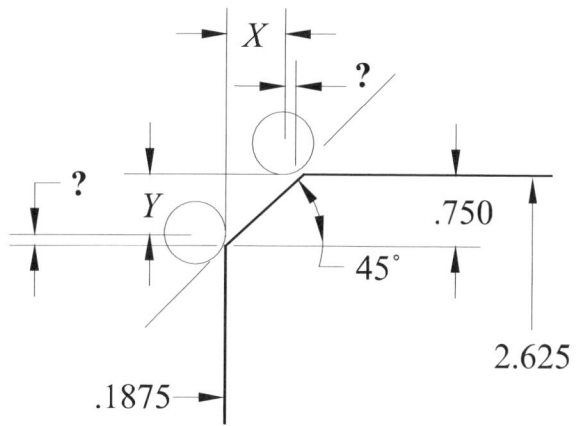

Figure 16
Calculate for Cutter Offset Coordinates

9. In Figure 17, a calculation is necessary to offset for the tool nose radius when turning a 30°-tapered surface. The face and centerline of the turned part are zero. List the coordinates needed in the CNC program, to allow for this offset.

Figure 17   Calculate for Tool Nose Radius Offset Coordinates

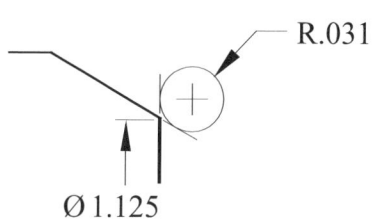

10. In Figure 18, a calculation is necessary to offset for the tool nose radius when turning a 30°-tapered surface. The face and centerline of the turned part are zero. List the coordinates needed in the CNC program, to allow for this offset.

Figure 18   Calculate for Tool Nose Radius Offset Coordinates

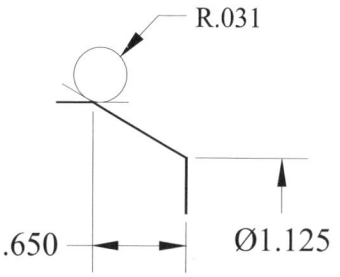

11. In Figure 19, a calculation is necessary to offset amount for the tool nose radius when turning a .062 inch 45° chamfer. The tool nose radius, in this case, is .015 inch. List the coordinates needed in the CNC program, to allow for this offset.

Figure 19   Calculate for Tool Nose Radius Offset
Coordinates

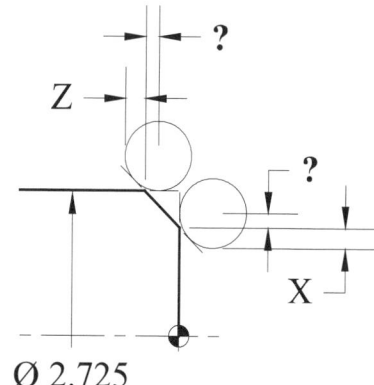

CNC Basics Study Questions

1. Programming is a method of defining tool movements through the application of numbers and corresponding coded letter symbols.
> T or F

2. A lathe has the following axes:
> a. X, Y & Z
> b. X & Y only
> c. X & Z only
> d. Y & Z only

3. Program coordinates that are based on a fixed origin are called:
> a. Incremental
> b. Absolute
> c. Relative
> d. Polar

4. On a two axis turning center, the diameter controlling axis is:
> a. B
> b. A
> c. X
> d. Z

5. The letter addresses used to identify axes of rotation are:
> a. U, V & W
> b. X, Y & Z
> c. A, Z & X
> d. A, B & C

6. The acronym TLO stands for:
> a. Tool Length Offset
> b. Total Length Offset
> c. Taper Length Offset
> d. Time Length Offset

7. When referring to the polar coordinate system, the clockwise rotation direction has a positive value.
> T or F

8. In the text "Programming of CNC Machines" Figure 15 of Part 1, which quadrant is the part placed in?

9. A program block is a single line of code followed by an end-of-block character.
         T or F

10. Each block contains one or more program words.
         T or F

11. Using Figure 13, Part 1, "Programming of CNC Machines", list the X and Y absolute coordinates for the part profile where workpiece zero is at the lower left corner. (The corner cutoff is at a 45° angle). Use a clockwise rotation direction.

12. Using Figure 13, in Part 1, "Programming of CNC Machines", list the X and Y incremental coordinates for the part profile where workpiece zero is at the lower left corner. Use a clockwise rotation direction.

13. How often should machine lubrication levels be checked?

SETUP AND OPERATION

In this section, the questions will require essay form answers. List your answers in the space provided, or attach a separate sheet if more space is needed. Please consult with your instructor and/or the answer key, at the end of this text, to review and compare your solutions with the suggested answers.

General Steps

1. What are the general steps required in order to prepare a CNC machine for production of a programmed part that has been effectively run before?

Operation Scenarios

2. When using the Pulse Generator (Handle) to move a selected axis for setup purposes, there are several increments available. List the incremental step magnitude for each:

3. What will occur when the reset button is pressed during automatic operation? What steps should be followed to recover?

4. What differences would exist when the Emergency Stop button is pressed during automatic operation, rather than the reset button and what will occur? What steps should be followed to recover?

5. When the Feed Hold button is pressed during automatic operation, what will occur? What steps should be followed to recover?

6. What mode of operation is required to install a tool into the spindle by the Automatic Tool Changer (ATC)?

    a. Automatic
    b. Jog
    c. Edit
    d. Manual Data Input (MDI)

7. It is highly advisable to conduct an in-process inspection of parts, as they are machined for the first time. What is the appropriate and safe method for performing these measurements?

8. If a part is machined on the lathe by tool #4 and it is found that the outside diameter measurement is oversize by .003, where, and how, is the change made to compensate for this variation?

9. If an existing wear offset is evident for tool #4 on the offset page of a lathe, what is the method for clearing this value so that no offset amount will remain?

10. In this case, the program execution has been interrupted. The tool that was being used is tool #6. How can the program be restarted from the beginning of that tool's use, and completed from that point on, rather than starting over at tool #1?

MDI Usage

11. Many times during the setup process, it is helpful to use Manual Data Input (MDI) to accomplish specific tasks. Name at least two of these tasks and explain how they would be useful. If possible, list the codes necessary to execute them.

Programming Editing

It is inevitable that program errors will happen and that program editing adjustments will be necessary. Answer the following questions with the procedures necessary to correct for this reality:

12. The program that is required calls for the G55 offset to be used on the CNC setup sheet. You have measured the offset data and entered it, at that location, on the offset page. When the program is loaded into active memory, it is noted on the program display that offset G54 is called in the program. Describe the course of action necessary to correct for this error.

13. The program you are using for the turning center does not include the tool or wear offset number for tool number 1. Describe the course of action necessary to insert the needed information into the program.

14. In the program, a comment (Date 03/30/07) is included. It is decided that it is not necessary to include this comment. Describe the course of action necessary to remove this portion of the program.

Setup and Operation Study Questions

1. The counterclockwise direction of rotation is always a negative axis movement when referring to the handle (pulse generator).
   > T or F

2. Which display includes the programmed Distance-to-Go readouts?

3. When the machine is ON and the program check screen is displayed, there is a list group of G-Codes displayed. What does this indicate?

4. Describe the difference between the Input and the +Input soft keys in the function.

5. Which button is used to activate automatic operation of a CNC program?
   > a. Emergency Stop
   > b. Cycle Stop
   > c. Cycle Start
   > d. Auto

6. Which display lists the CNC program?
   > a. Position page
   > b. Offset page
   > c. Program check
   > d. Program page

7. When the machine is turned on for the first time, it must be sent to its home position.
   > T or F

8. Which operation selection button allows for the execution of a single CNC command?
   > a. Dry run
   > b. Single block
   > c. Block delete
   > d. Optional stop

9. Which mode switch/button enables the operator to make changes to the program?
   > a. Edit
   > b. MDI
   > c. Auto
   > d. Jog

10. What does the acronym MDI stand for?

11. Which display screen is used to enter tool information?

12. If the Reset button is pressed during automatic operation, spindle rotations, feed and coolant will stop.

                    T or F

13. During setup, the mode switch used to allow for manual movement of the machine axes is:

        a. Auto
        b. MDI
        c. Edit
        d. Jog

CNC TURNING CENTER PROGRAMMING

CNC Turning Center Program Template

The following program template can be used as a guide for inputting the data necessary to create a program. Make copies to complete each program exercise, or use a separate lined sheet of paper. Certain sections of the machining program can be repetitious in nature and they are listed here as follows: the program beginning, the tool beginning, the tool ending and the program ending. Note: If you intend to load any of the programs you create into a machine controller for trial and use, you must include a percent (%) sign on a separate line at the beginning and end of the text. This is required for communications purposes. The program block structure for each of these sections is:

The Program Beginning

O7306 = program number
(Comments) = part number or other identifying information
(Comments) = date or other identifying information
Note: 9000 series program numbering is reserved for Macro programs; therefore, avoid using it for your program number.

The Tool Beginning

(Comments) = tool identification information
N100T????
N105G96S???M03
N110G00X????Z????M08

The Tool Ending

N200G00G40X????Z.1M09
N205G28U0W0T??00
N210M01

The Program Ending

N300G28U0W0M09
N305M30

    Note: the question marks in the above template will be replaced with live data that is relevant to your programming situation.

The following G and M-Code reference charts are given to aid in the programming process.

Preparatory Functions (G-Codes)   Specific to CNC Turning Centers

Code	Group	Function
*G00	01	Rapid Traverse Positioning
G01	01	Linear Interpolation
G02	01	Circular and Helical Interpolation CW (clockwise)
G03	01	Circular and Helical Interpolation CCW (counterclockwise)
G04	00	Dwell
G09	00	Exact Stop
G10	00	Data Setting
G20	06	Input in Inches
G21	06	Input in Millimeters
*G22	09	Stored Stroke Limit ON
G23	09	Stored Stroke Limit OFF
G25	08	Spindle Speed Fluctuation Detection ON
G26	08	Spindle Speed Fluctuation Detection OFF
G27	00	Reference Point Return Check
G28	00	Reference Point Return
G29	00	Return From Reference Point
G30	00	Return to Second, Third, and Fourth Reference Point
G32	01	Thread Cutting
*G40	07	Tool Nose Radius Compensation Cancel
G41	07	Tool Nose Radius Compensation, Left Side
G42	07	Tool Nose Radius Compensation, Right Side
G50	00	Coordinate System Setting/ Maximum Spindle Speed Setting
G52	00	Local Coordinate System Setting
G53	00	Machine Coordinate System Setting
G54	14	Work Coordinate System One Selection
G68	04	Mirror Image for Double Turrets ON
*G69	04	Mirror Image for Double Turrets OFF
G70	00	Finishing Cycle
G71	00	Stock Removal in Turning
G72	00	Stock Removal in Facing
G73	00	Pattern Repeating
G74	00	Peck Drilling Cycle
G75	00	Groove Cutting Cycle
G76	00	Multiple Thread Cutting Cycle
*G80	10	Canned Drilling Cycle Cancellation
G83	10	Face Drilling Cycle
G84	10	Face Tapping Cycle
G86	10	Face Boring Cycle
G90	01	Outer/Inner Diameter Turning Cycle
G92	01	Thread Cutting Cycle
G94	01	Face Cutting Cycle
G96	02	Constant Surface Speed Control
*G97	02	Constant Surface Speed Control Cancellation
G98	05	Feed per Minute
*G99	05	Feed per Revolution

Miscellaneous Functions, M-Codes for CNC Turning

M-Code	Function
M00	Program Stop
M01	Optional Stop
M02	Program End Without Rewind
M03	Spindle ON Clockwise (CW) Rotation
M04	Spindle ON Counterclockwise (CCW) Rotation
M05	Spindle OFF Rotation Stop
M08	Flood Coolant ON
M09	Coolant OFF
M10	Chuck Close
M11	Chuck Open
M12	Tailstock Quill Advance
M13	Tailstock Quill Retract
M17	Rotation of Tool Turret Forward
M18	Rotation of Tool Turret Backward
M21	Tailstock Direction Forward
M22	Tailstock Direction Backward
M23	Threading Finishing with Chamfering
M24	Threading Finishing with Right-Angle
M30	Program End With Rewind
M41	Spindle LOW Gear Range Command
M42	Spindle HIGH Gear Range Command
M71	Bar Feed ON – Start
M72	Bar Feed OFF – Stop
M73	Parts Catcher Advance
M74	Parts Catcher Retract
M98	Subroutine Call
M99	Return to Main Program From Subroutine

The following Turning Center Programming Sheet can be used as a guide for inputting the data necessary to create a program. Make copies to complete each program exercise or use a separate lined sheet of paper.

CNC Machining Center
Programming Sheet

Date:					Prepared By:					
Part Name:					Part Number:					
Machine:					Program Number:					
Line #	Preparatory	X Axis Coordinate	Y Axis Coordinate	Z Axis Coordinate	Modifiers	Feed Rate	Tool #	Offset #	Spindle Speed	M Codes

CNC Turning Center Tool List

The following diagrams identify the tools to choose from for planning your programs. Note that there is only one tool # for a Center Drill and for a specific drill size. There will undoubtedly be additional locations on the turret for drilling tools.

Rough Turning, Tool #1
.031 Nose Radius

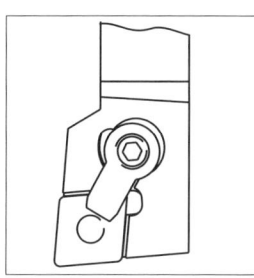

Finish Turning, Tool #2
.015 Nose Radius

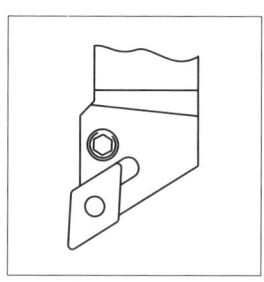

Rough Boring, Tool #3
.031 Nose Radius

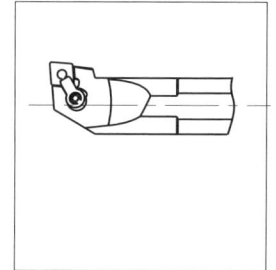

Finish Boring, Tool #4
.015 Nose Radius

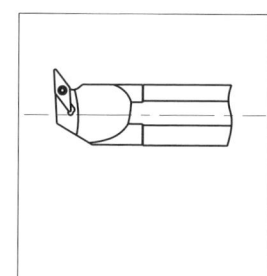

OD Grooving, Tool #5
156 Wide .005 Nose Radius

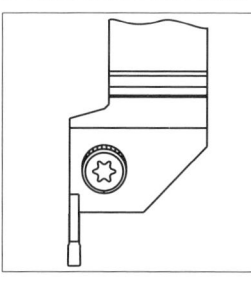

ID Grooving, Tool #6
.156 Wide .005 Nose Radius

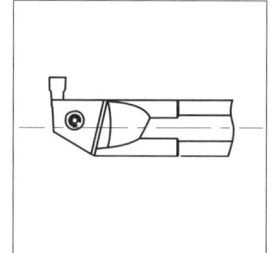

OD Threading, Tool #7

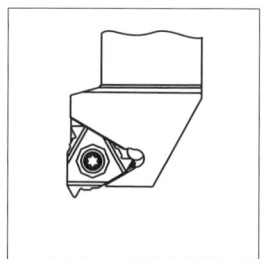

ID Threading, Tool #8

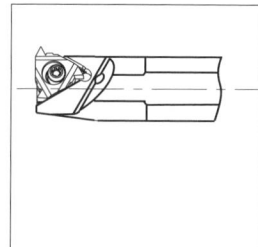

#3 Center Drill, Tool #9

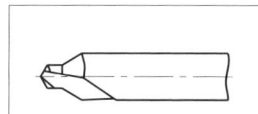

#5 Center Drill, Tool #9

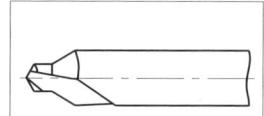

Specific Diameter Drill,
Tool #10

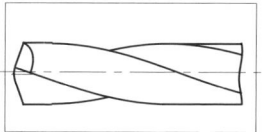

Programming Coordinate Identification for Turning

1. For the drawing below, identify and list the programming coordinate points (indicated by the small filled dots), for the part contour using absolute dimensioning. The face of the part (right end) and centerline are the part zero location. Please list all values for the X-axis as radial values and include the arc center locations for programming of the arcs.

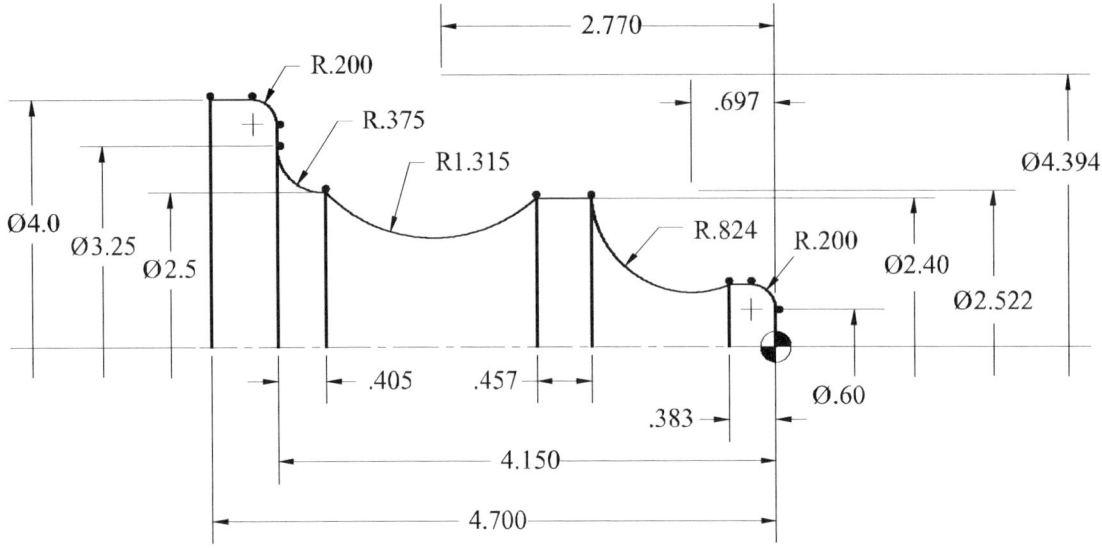

Figure 20 Identify the Absolute and Incremental Coordinates

2. Using the same drawing, identify and list the programming coordinate points for the part contour using incremental dimensioning. Please list all values for the X-axis as radial values and include the incremental arc center values.

Linear Interpolation

Simple Turning Exercises

CNC Turning Center Programming Exercise 1

Using linear interpolation, write a program to create the tool path for the contour, in one depth of cut pass, for the following drawing. The material is stainless steel. For this and all of the remaining exercises, set the r/min to Constant Surface Speed (G96) and use the chart to determine a midrange value. Set the in/rev for feed rate to a midrange value also. For this and the remainder of all examples, you should list the X-axis values as diametrical values. The dashed line on the drawing indicates the net shape of the part and the metal to be removed.

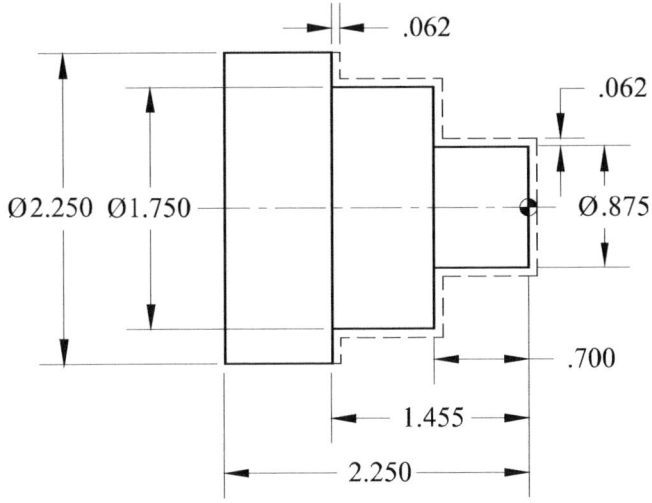

.062

.062

Ø2.250   Ø1.750

Ø.875

Figure 21 Turning Center Programming Exercise 1

.700

1.455

2.250

Caution: DO NOT attempt to execute this program from solid bar stock.

CNC Turning Center Programming Exercise 2

Using linear interpolation, write a program to create the tool path for the contour, in one depth-of-cut pass, for the following drawing. Please use any calculations necessary to offset the tool path for the Tool Nose Radius Compensation (TNRC). The material is alloy steel. <u>The dashed line on the drawing indicates the net shape of the part and the metal to be removed.</u>
    Caution: DO NOT attempt to execute this program from solid bar stock.

CNC Turning Center Programming Exercise 3

Using the Fixed Cutting Cycle B (G94), write a program to create the facing cut for the following drawing (Figure 23) in 3 equal depths of cut passes. The material is stainless steel.

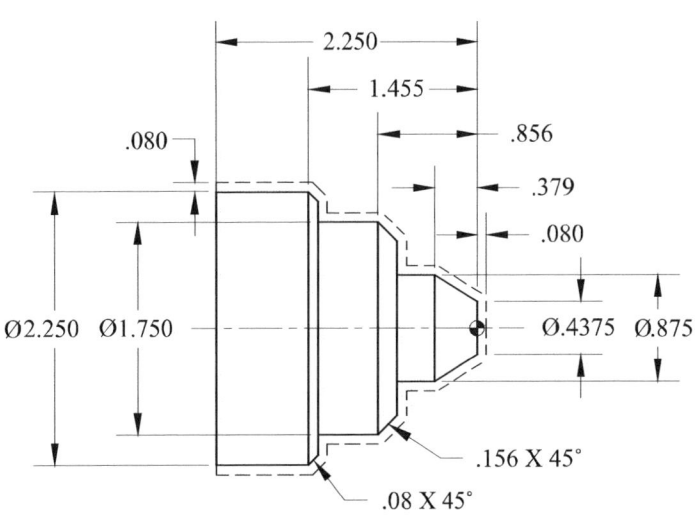

2.250

1.455

.080

.856

.379

.080

Ø2.250   Ø1.750

Ø.4375   Ø.875

.156 X 45°

.08 X 45°

Figure 22 Turning Center Programming Exercise 2

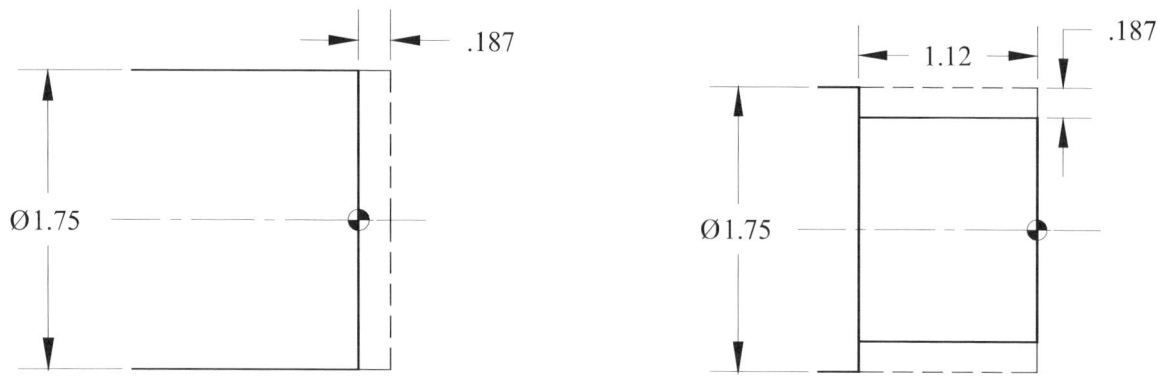

Figure 23 Turning Center Programming Exercise 3   **Figure 24 Turning Center Programming Exercise 4**

CNC Turning Center Programming Exercise 4

Using the Fixed Cutting Cycle A (G90), write a program to create the turning cut for the drawing (Figure 24) in 3 equal depth of cut passes. The material is stainless steel.

Linear and Circular Interpolation

CNC Turning Center Programming Exercise 5

Using linear and circular interpolation, write a program to create the tool path for the contour of the following drawing. Please use any calculations necessary to offset the tool path to allow for Tool Nose Radius Compensation (TNRC). Do Not use G41 or G42 in this exercise. The material is aluminum. The machine being used has a maximum spindle r/min of 6000. <u>The dashed line on the drawing indicates the net shape of the part and the metal to be removed.</u>
Caution: DO NOT attempt to execute this program from solid bar stock.

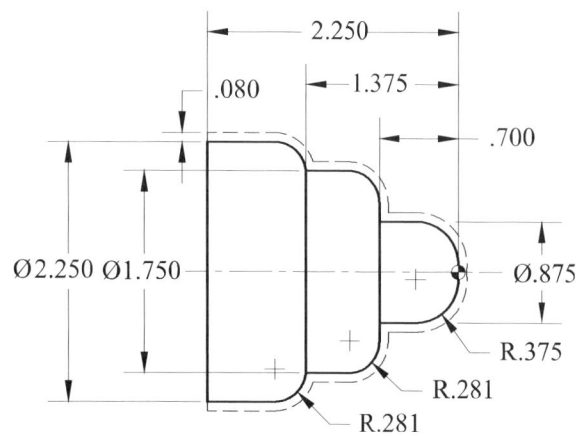

Figure 25
Turning Center Programming Exercise 5

CNC Turning Center Programming Exercise 6

Using linear and circular interpolation, write a program to create the tool path for the contour of the following drawing. Please use any calculations necessary to offset the tool path for Tool Nose Radius Compensation (TNRC). Do Not use G41 or G42 in this exercise. The material is aluminum. <u>The dashed line on the drawing indicates the net shape of the part and the metal to be removed.</u>

Caution: DO NOT attempt to execute this program from solid bar stock.

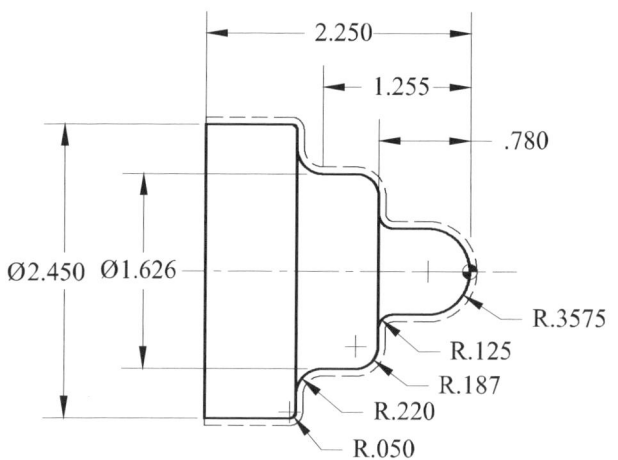

Figure 26
Turning Center Programming Exercise 6

Tool Nose Radius Compensation

CNC Turning Center Programming Exercise 7

Exercise 2 with TNRC

Now use the appropriate Tool Nose Radius Compensation (TNRC) G40, G41 and/or G42 for the tool path contours in exercises 2, 5 and 6. For the remainder of all examples you should use the appropriate TNRC. <u>The dashed line on the drawing indicates the net shape of the part and the metal to be removed.</u>

Caution: DO NOT attempt to execute this program from solid bar stock.

CNC Turning Center Programming Exercise 8

Exercise 5 with TNRC

<u>The dashed line on the drawing indicates the net shape of the part and the metal to be removed.</u>

Caution: DO NOT attempt to execute this program from solid bar stock.

CNC Turning Center Programming Exercise 9

Exercise 6 with TNRC

The dashed line on the drawing indicates the net shape of the part and the metal to be removed.

Caution: DO NOT attempt to execute this program from solid bar stock.

Drilling

CNC Turning Center Programming Exercise 10

In this example, it is necessary to center drill the part in order to prepare for subsequent drilling. The material is stainless steel and the finished hole should be countersunk to a .405 inch diameter. Calculate the required depth for the center drill and program the tool path using G01.

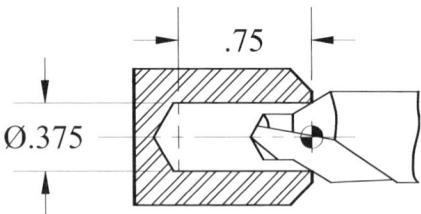

Figure 27
Turning Center Programming
Exercise 10

CNC Turning Center Programming Exercise 11

G74 Drilling Cycle

To finish the hole as described in example ten, it is necessary to drill to the depth as shown in the following drawing. The material is stainless steel and the G74 drilling cycle should be used with 3 equal depth cuts.

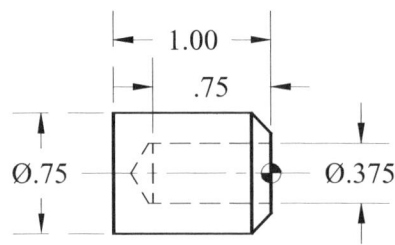

Figure 28
Turning Center Programming
Exercise 11

Multiple Repetitive Cycles

CNC Turning Center Programming Exercise 12

G71 & G70 Rough and Finish Turn Cycle

The part in the drawing below needs to be rough and finish turned to specifications. Use the G71 and G70 Turning Cycles to accomplish this. In this case, the material is aluminum. Set the roughing depth of cut at .08 inch and the finish allowance for the X-axis at .015 inch and .005

inch on the Z-axis. The cut on the face of the part of .031 of excess material should be done in one pass. Make any calculations necessary to program the tool path and write the program.

Figure 29 Turning Center Programming Exercise 12

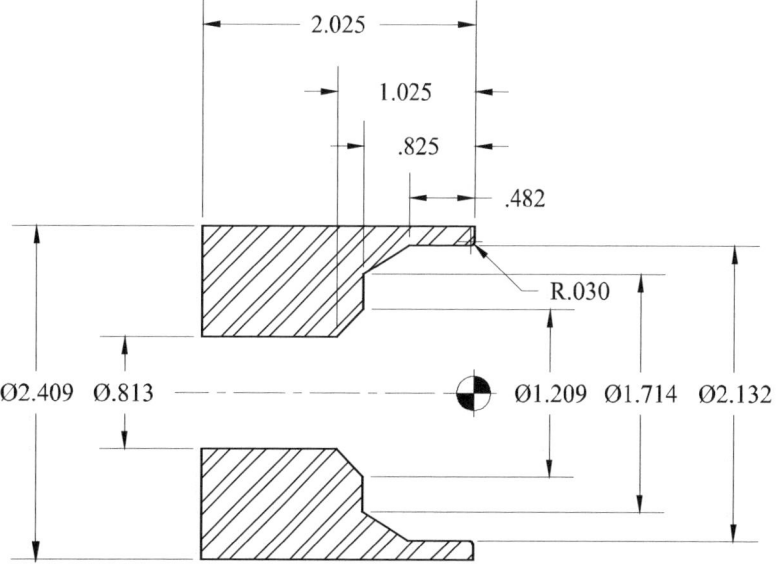

Boring

CNC Turning Center Programming Exercise 13

G71 & G70 Rough and Finish Turn Cycle

The same Rough and Finish Turning Cycles may be applied to internal boring. Write a program for the following drawing using these cycles. The material is aluminum and the .813 inch diameter hole already exists in the part. Set the rough depth of cut at .08 inch and the finish allowance at .015 inch and .005 inch on the Z-axis. Make any calculations necessary to program the tool path and write the program, including any preparatory machining necessary.

Figure 30 Turning Center Programming Exercise 13

CNC Turning Center Programming Exercise 14

G72 Face Cutting Cycle

Occasionally, the part geometry will dictate the method of machining. The following case is one instance. The part in the drawing below needs to be faced using the G72 Face Cutting Cycle. In this case, the material is aluminum. Set the roughing depth of cut at .06 inch and the finish allowance at .015 inch. Make any calculations necessary to program the tool path and write the program.

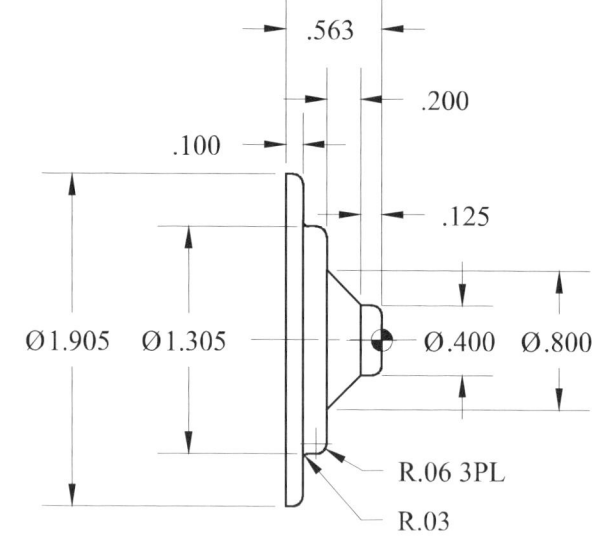

Figure 31 Turning Center Programming Exercise 14

CNC Turning Center Programming Exercise 15

G73 Pattern
Repeating Cycle

The part in the drawing below has a net shape that needs a specific amount of material removed from all surfaces. Use the G73 turning cycle to accomplish this. In this case, the material is stainless steel. Set the number of roughing passes at three and the finish allowance at .03 inch. Make any calculations necessary to program the tool path and write the program. <u>The dashed line on the drawing indicates the net shape of the part and the metal to be removed.</u>

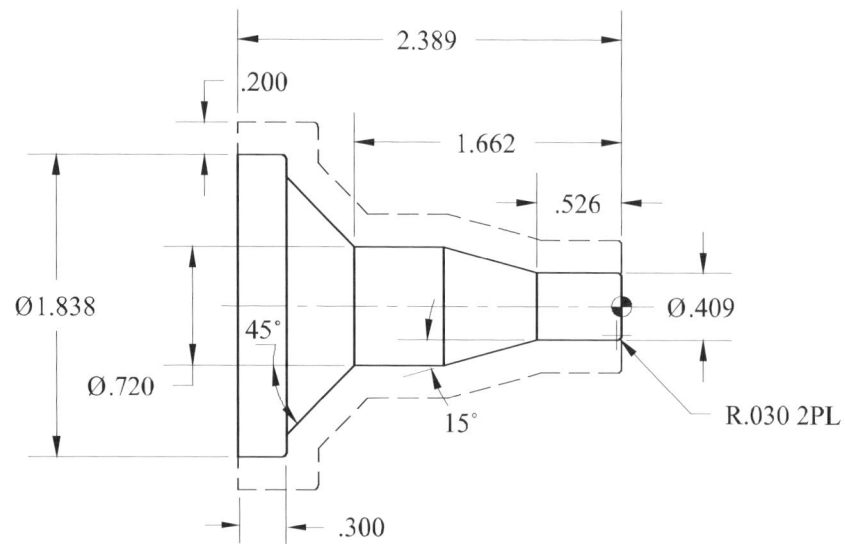

Figure 32 Turning Center Programming Exercise 15

Caution: DO NOT attempt to execute this program from solid bar stock.

CNC Turning Center Programming Exercise 16

The same situation applies to a case of internal boring. Write a program for the following drawing using the G73 cycle. The material is stainless steel. Set the number of roughing passes at three and the finish allowance at .03 inch. Make any calculations necessary to program the tool·path and write the program. <u>The dashed line on the drawing indicates the net shape of the part and the metal to be removed.</u> The .813 diameter has been predrilled in an earlier operation.
Caution: DO NOT attempt to execute this program from solid bar stock.

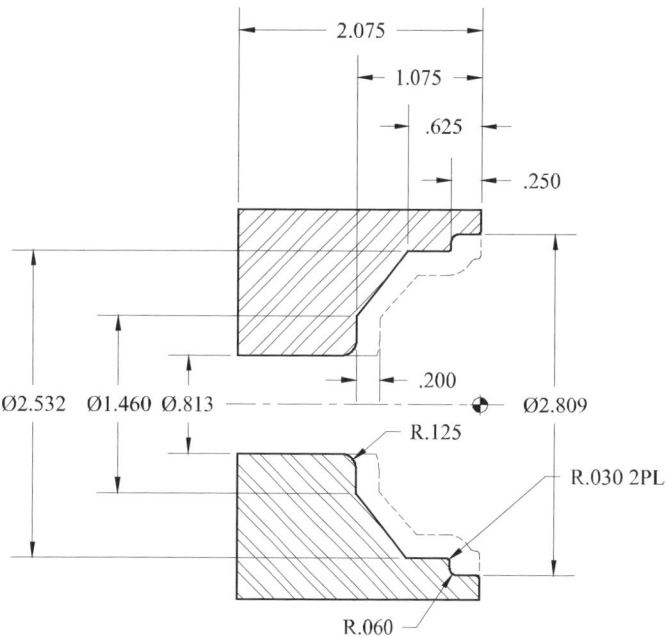

Figure 33
Turning Center Programming Exercise 16

Grooving

CNC Turning Center Programming Exercise 17

G75 Grooving Cycle

A common operation prior to threading is the creation of an escape groove at the end of the threads. Use the information in the following drawing to write a program to machine the groove using the G75 cycle. The material is carbon steel.

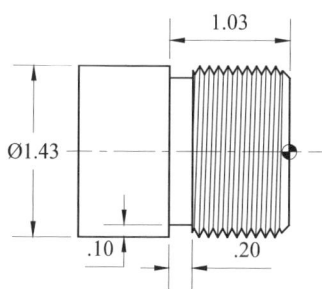

Figure 34
Turning Center Programming Exercise 17

OD Threading

CNC Turning Center Programming Exercise 18

G76 Threading Cycle

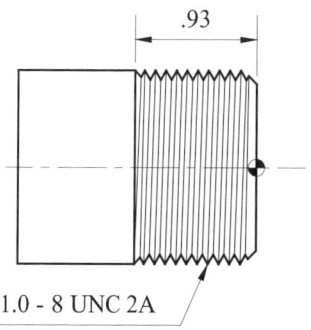

Figure 35   Turning Center Programming Exercise 18

Write a program to machine the threaded portion on the part in the following drawing, using the G76 threading cycle. The material is carbon steel bar stock of 1.0 inch diameter.

CNC Turning Center Subprogram Application

CNC Turning Center Programming Exercise 19

M98 and M99

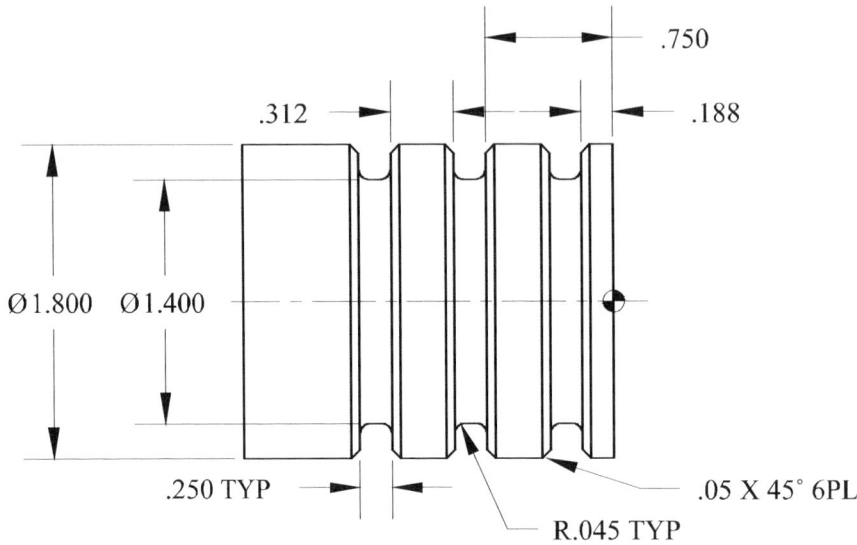

Figure 36　Turning Center Programming Exercise 19

　　　Use linear and circular interpolation to create the programmed tool path for the grooves shown in the drawing below. You should make the groove geometry in a subprogram and then call it for each groove location from the main program. The material for this project is aluminum.

CNC Turning Center Combined Project

CNC Turning Center Programming Exercise 20

　　　In the Process Planning section of this workbook, you identified the operation, tools and setup information for this part. Now use the information that you gathered to write a program for the same part. Note: the OD should be roughed and then finished with separate tools.

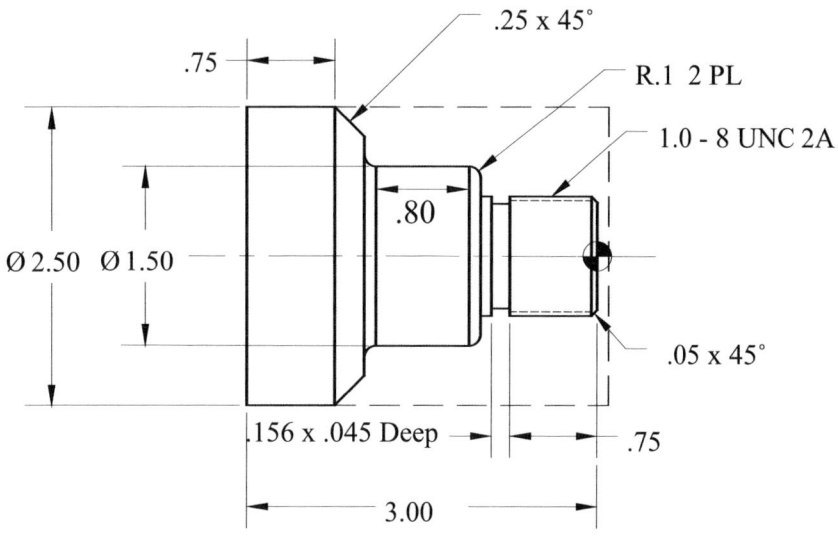

Figure 37 Turning Center Programming Exercise 20

CNC Turning Center Program Diagnosis

Use the skills you have learned to identify the problems in the following program lines and program sections. You may refer to the text, "Programming of CNC Machines" Third Edition.

1. Use the following CNC code and sketch a representation of the part that would be machined.

```
O2001
(CNC Turning Center Program Diagnosis, Problem 1)
(Tool #1, Rough Turning Tool)
N10G50S2000
N15T0100M42
N20G96S500M03
N25G00X2.2Z.3T0101M08
N30G01Z.01F.03
N35X0.F.012
N40G00X3.0Z.2
N45G73P50Q85I.168K.169U.04W.02D3F.012
N50G00X1.59
N55G01Z0
N60X1.75Z-.08
N65Z-1.375
```

N70X2.0W-.125
N75Z-2.1
N80G03U.3Z-2.25I-.15K0.F.004
N85G01X2.85
N90G28U0W0T0100
N95M30

2. Find the error in this program line.

N100G03U.3Z-2.25F.004

3. Find the error in following program lines.

O2003
(CNC Turning Center Program Diagnosis, Problem 3)
(Tool 9 = #5 Center Drill)
N10T0900
N20G97S641M03
N30G00X0Z.1T0909M08
N40G1Z-.4303
N50G0Z.1M09
N60G28U0W0T0900
N70M30

4. Find the error in the following program section.

O2004
(CNC Turning Center Program Diagnosis, Problem 4)
(Tool #1, Rough Turning Tool)
N10T0100
N20G50S6000
N30G96S3650
N40G00X0Z.1T0101M08
. . . .
. . . .

5. Find the error in the following program.

O2005
(CNC Turning Center Program Diagnosis, Problem 5)

(Tool #3, Rough Boring Tool)
N10T0300
N20G50S6000
N30G96S2800M3
N40G0G41X.713Z.1T0303M08
N50G71U.08R.03
N60G71P50Q150U.015W.005
N70G0X2.192
N80G01Z0F.0265
N90G2X2.132Z-.03R.03
N100G01Z-.482
N110X1.714Z-.825
N120X1.209
N130X.813Z-1.025
N140X.713
N150G28G40U0W0T0300
N160M01

6. Find the error in the following program section.

O2006
(CNC Turning Center Program Diagnosis, Problem 6)
(Tool #1, Rough Turning Tool)
N10T0100
N20G96S563M03
N30G00G41X.6975Z.1M08
N40G1Z0F.022
N50X-.01
N60G0Z.1
N70G42X.4375

. . . .
. . . .

7. Find the error in the following program.

O2007
(CNC Turning Center Program Diagnosis, Problem 7)
(Tool #1, Rough Turning Tool)
N10T0100
N20G96S563M03
N30G00G41X.6975Z.1T0101M08

N40G1Z0F.022
N50X-.01
N60G0Z.1
N70X.4375
N80G1Z0
N90X.875Z-.379
N100Z-.7
N110X1.438
N120X1.75Z-.856
N130Z-1.375
N140X2.09
N150X2.25Z-1.455
N160Z-2.25
N170G0X2.35Z.1M09
N180G28G40U0W0
N190M30

8. Find the error in the following program section.

O2008
(CNC Turning Center Program Diagnosis, Problem 8)
(Tool #1, Rough Turning Tool)
N10T0100
N20G50S6000
N30G96S2800M3
N40G0G42X2.005Z.1T0101M08
N50G72U.06R.1
N60G72P70Q190U.015W.015
N70G0Z0F.0265
N80X.28
N90G3X.4Z-.06R.06
N100Z-.125F.0265
N110X.8Z-.325
N120X1.185
N130G3X1.305Z-.385R.06
N140G01Z-.433
N150G2X1.365Z-.463R.03
N160G1X1.785
N170G3X1.905Z-.523R.06
N180G01Z-.563

N190X2.005
N200G28G40U0W0T0100
N210M01

9. Find the error in the following program section.

(Tool #2, Finish Turning Tool)
N220T0200
N230G50S6000
N240G96M3
N250G0G42X.90Z.1T0202M08
N260G70P80Q190
N270G28G40U0W0T0200M09
N280M30

10. Find the error in the following program section.

(Tool #4, Finish Boring Tool)
N170T0400
N180G50S6000
N190G96S2800M3
N200G0G42X.90Z.1T0404M08
N210G70P80Q140
N220G28U0W0T0400M09
N230M30

CNC MACHINING CENTER PROGRAMMING

CNC Machining Center Program Template

Certain sections of the machining program can be repetitious in nature and they are listed here, as follows: the program beginning, the safety block, the tool beginning, the tool ending and the program ending. *Note: If you intend to load any of the programs you create into a machine controller for trial and use, you must include a percent (%) sign on a separate line at the beginning and end of the text. This is required for communications purposes.* The program block structure for each of these sections is:

The Program Beginning

O2406 = program number
(Comments) = part number or other identifying information
(Comments) = date or other identifying information
Note: 9000 series program numbering is reserved for Macro programs; therefore, avoid using it for your program number
N10G90G20G80G40G49
The Safety Block
(See EXPLANATION OF THE SAFETY BLOCK in "Programming of CNC Machines", Third Edition, Part 4, Programming of CNC Machining Centers, for complete details).

The Tool Beginning

(Comments) = tool identification information
N20T01M06
N25S1000M03
N30G54G0X0.0Y0.0
N35G43Z1.0H01
N40Z.1M08
Note: The tool number (T01) and tool height offset number (H01), the value entered in your program for spindle r/min (S), and the values entered n your programs for X and Y coordinates listed with G54, will vary dependant the specific application.

The Tool Ending

N100G80Z.1M09
N105G91G28Z0
N110M01

The Program Ending

N200X0Y0

N205M30

Note: the coordinate points in line N30 of the above template will be replaced with live data that is relevant to your programming situation.

The following G and M-Code reference charts are given to aid in the programming process.

Preparatory Functions (G-Codes) specific to Machining Centers

Code	Group	Function
*G00	01	Rapid Traverse Positioning
*G01	01	Linear Interpolation
G02	01	Circular and Helical Interpolation CW (Clockwise)
G03	01	Circular and Helical Interpolation CCW (Counterclockwise)
G04	00	Dwell
G09	00	Exact Stop
G10	00	Data Setting
*G15	17	Polar Coordinates Cancellation
G16	17	Polar Coordinates System
*G17	02	XY Plane Selection
G18	02	ZX Plane Selection
G19	02	YZ Plane Selection
G20	06	Input in Inches
G21	06	Input in Millimeters
*G22	04	Stored Stroke Limit ON
G23	04	Stored Stroke Limit OFF
G27	00	Reference Position Return Check
G28	00	Reference Position Return
G29	00	Return From Reference Position
G30	00	Return to Second, Third, and Fourth Reference Position
G33	01	Thread Cutting
G37	00	Automatic Tool Length Measurement
*G40	07	Cutter Compensation Cancel
G41	07	Cutter Compensation Left Side
G42	07	Cutter Compensation Right Side
G43	08	Tool length Offset Compensation Positive (+) Direction
G44	08	Tool Length Offset Compensation Negative (-) Direction
G45	00	Tool Offset Increase
G46	00	Tool Offset Decrease
G47	00	Tool Offset Double Increase
G48	00	Tool Offset Double Decrease
*G49	08	Tool Length Offset Compensation Cancel
*G50	11	Scaling Cancel
G51	11	Scaling
G52	00	Local Coordinate System
G53	00	Machine Coordinate System

Preparatory Functions (G-Codes) specific to Machining Centers, continued

Code	Group	Function
*G54	14	Work Coordinate System 1
G55	14	Work Coordinate System 2
G56	14	Work Coordinate System 3
G57	14	Work Coordinate System 4
G58	14	Work Coordinate System 5
G59	14	Work Coordinate System 6
G60	00	Single Direction Positioning
G63	15	Tapping Mode
G68	16	Rotation of Coordinate System
*G69	16	Cancellation of Coordinate System Rotation
G73	09	High Speed Peck Drilling Cycle
G74	09	Reverse Tapping Cycle
G76	09	Fine Boring Cycle
*G80	09	Canned Cycle Cancel
G81	09	Drilling Cycle, Spot Drilling
G82	09	Drilling Cycle, Counter Boring
G83	09	Deep Hole Drilling Cycle
G84	09	Tapping Cycle
G85	09	Reaming Cycle
G86	09	Boring Cycle
G87	09	Back Boring Cycle
G88	09	Boring Cycle
G89	09	Boring Cycle
*G90	03	Absolute Programming Command
*G91	03	Incremental Programming Command
G92	00	Setting for the Work Coordinate System or Maximum Spindle r/min
*G94	05	Feed per Minute
G95	05	Feed per Revolution
G96	13	Constant Surface Speed Control
*G97	13	Constant Surface Speed Control Cancel
*G98	10	Canned Cycle Initial Level Return
G99	10	Canned Cycle R-Level Return

Miscellaneous Functions, M-Codes for Machining Centers

Code	Function
M00	Program Stop
M01	Optional Stop
M02	Program End Without Rewind
M03	Spindle ON Clockwise (CW) Rotation
M04	Spindle ON Counterclockwise (CCW) Rotation
M05	Spindle OFF Rotation Stop
M06	Tool Change
M07	Mist Coolant ON
M08	Flood Coolant ON
M09	Coolant OFF
M10	Work Table Rotation Locked
M11	Work Table Rotation Unlocked
M13	Spindle ON Clockwise and Coolant ON, Dual Command
M14	Spindle ON Counterclockwise and Coolant ON, Dual Command
M16	Change of Heavy Tools
M19	Spindle Orientation
M21	Mirror Image in the Direction of the X Axis
M22	Mirror Image in the Direction of the Y Axis
M23	Cancellation of the Mirror Image
M30	Program End with Rewind
M98	Subprogram Call
M99	Return to Main Program from Subprogram

The following CNC Machining Center Programming Sheet can be used as a guide for inputting the data necessary to create a program. Make as many copies as are needed to complete each program exercise, or use a separate lined sheet of paper.

**CNC Machining Center
Programming Sheet**

Date:					Prepared By:					
Part Name:					Part Number:					
Machine:					Program Number:					
Line #	Preparatory	X Axis Coordinate	Y Axis Coordinate	Z Axis Coordinate	Modifiers	Feed Rate	Tool #	Offset #	Spindle Speed	M Codes

CNC Machining Center Tool List

The following list identifies the tools that are available to choose from for planning your programs. For these exercises, the tool carousel on the CNC Machining Center you are programming holds up to 30 tools and the diameter offset value is to be identified with #'s 31-60, corresponding with the tool (i.e. T1 = D31). In the following exercises, where only one tool is required, a CNC Setup sheet is not necessary, but the tool and setup information should be listed before your program code. Please use a CNC Setup sheet in all other cases, for the sake of clarity.

Face Mill, 3.0 inch diameter, 90°, 5 teeth, Carbide

End Mill, 2-Flute, 1/8 inch
End Mill, 2-Flute, 3/8 inch
End Mill, 2-Flute, 9/16 inch
End Mill, 2-Flute, 1.0 inch

End Mill, 4-Flute, 3/8 inch
End Mill, 4-Flute, 1/2 inch
End Mill, 4-Flute, 5/8 inch
End Mill, 4-Flute, 3/4 inch
End Mill, 4-Flute, 1.0 inch

Roughing End Mill, 4-Flute, 1.0 inch

#5 Center Drill
#6 Center Drill
Spotting Drill, .75 diameter, 90° single flute
Drill Bits, All sets are available in High Speed Steel
Taps, All sizes are available in High Speed Steel
Reamers, all required sizes are available in High Speed Steel

Programming Coordinate Identification for Milling

1. Use the drawing (Figure 38) to identify the points on the profile geometry using absolute dimensioning to program the part. Include the arc center locations. Start at the zero location of the part and proceed clockwise until all points are identified.

2. Use the drawing (Figure 38) to identify the points on the profile geometry using incremental dimensioning to program the part. Include the arc center locations. Start at the zero location of the part and proceed clockwise until all points are identified.

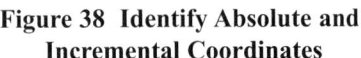

Figure 38 Identify Absolute and Incremental Coordinates

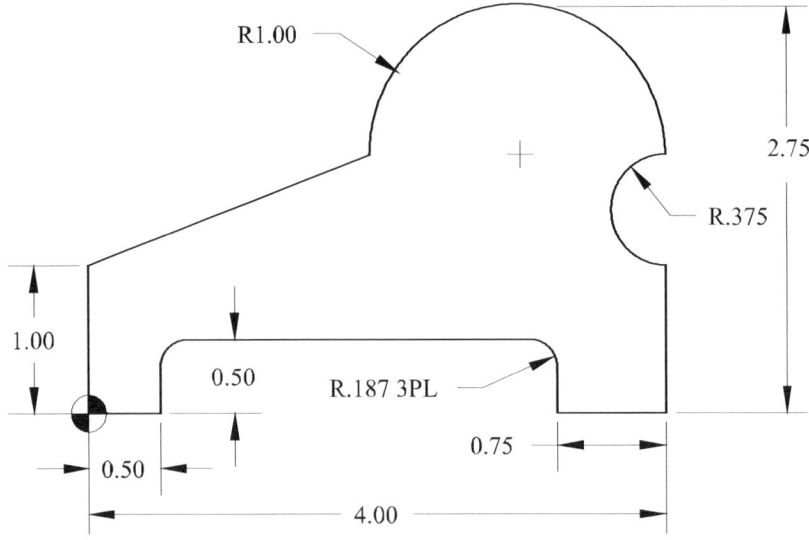

R1.00

2.75

R.375

1.00

0.50

R.187 3PL

0.50

0.75

4.00

Linear Interpolation on the CNC Machining Center

In each of the following examples, if only one tool is needed to complete the part, a CNC Setup Sheet is not required. Please list the tool to be used, the Cutting Speed range, the r/min range, the in/tooth range and the in/min range, where appropriate. Choose the mid range values for feeds and speeds to input into your programs.

Face Milling Exercises

CNC Machining Center Exercise #1

Using G00 and G01, program the moves required to face off .08 inch from the face of this part. The material is Alloy Steel.

Figure 39
Machining Center Programming Exercise 1

4.25

2.00

CNC Machining Center Exercise #2

Using G00 and G01, program the moves required to face off .07 inch from the face of this part. Use single directional cutting. The material is Aluminum.

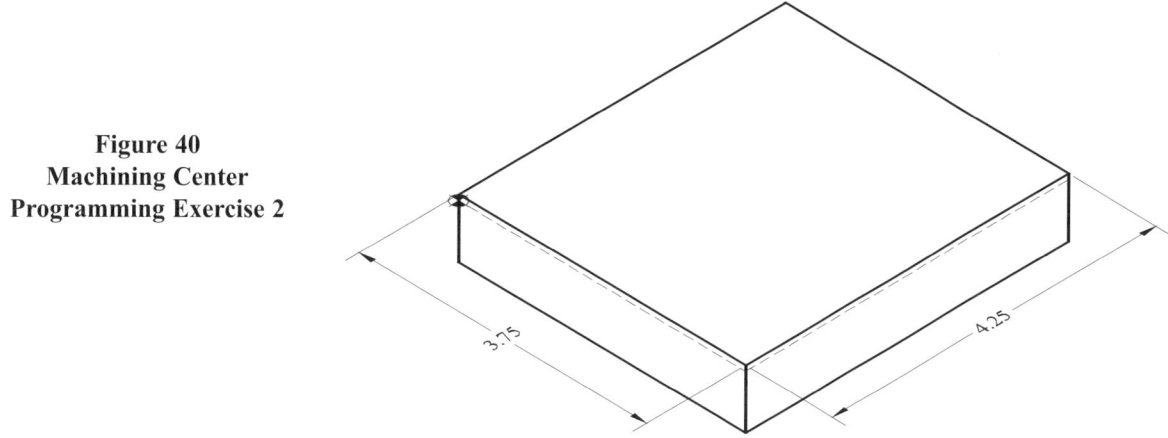

Figure 40
Machining Center
Programming Exercise 2

Contour Milling

CNC Machining Center Exercise #3

Using G00 and G01, program the moves required to mill the contour of this part. Use a .375 inch diameter 4 fluted (HSS) end mill and climb mill directional cutting for this example. The material is Alloy Steel and the part zero is located in the upper left hand corner of the part. To machine the step will require two depth of cut passes.

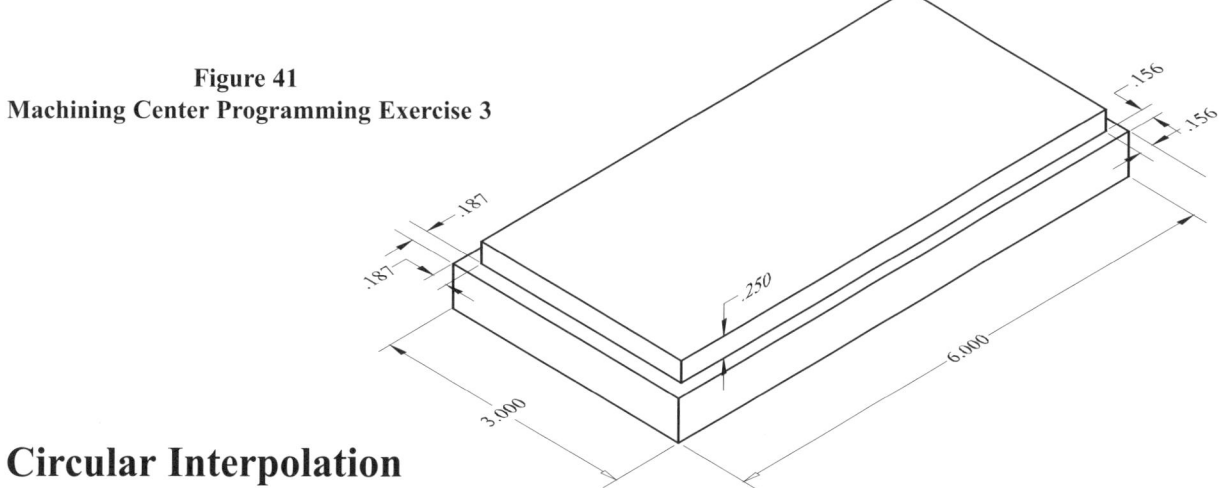

Figure 41
Machining Center Programming Exercise 3

Circular Interpolation

CNC Machining Center Exercise #4

Using G01, G02, or G03, program the moves required to mill the contour of this part. To enable cutting of the entire step in one axial pass, you will need to make a calculation to select the correct minimum diameter end mill. Use climb mill directional cutting for this example. For a minimum of two out of four of the radii, you must use the I and J commands for programming.

The material is Alloy Steel. The depth of the step is .375 inch and it should be machined in two equal depth of cut passes. The overall part thickness is 1.0 inch.

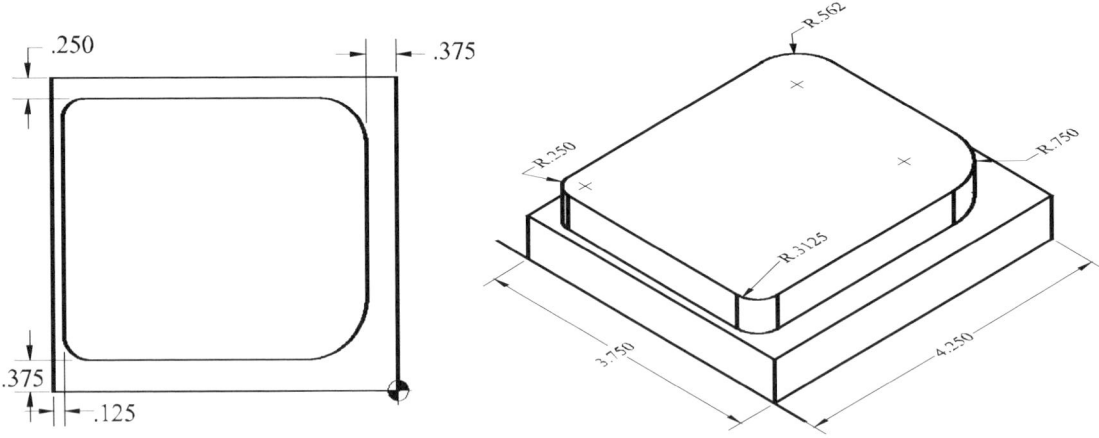

Figure 42 Machining Center Programming Exercise 4

CNC Machining Center Exercise #5

Using G01, G02, or G03, program the moves required to mill the contour of this part. You will need to make a calculation to properly offset the cutter for the angular cut. End mill selection will be dictated by the fillet radius requirements on the profile of the part. You will need to use climb mill directional cutting. For a minimum of two out of four of the radii, you must use the I and J commands. The material is Aluminum and the thickness of the part is .500 inch. In this case, the maximum r/min of the machine being used is 6000.

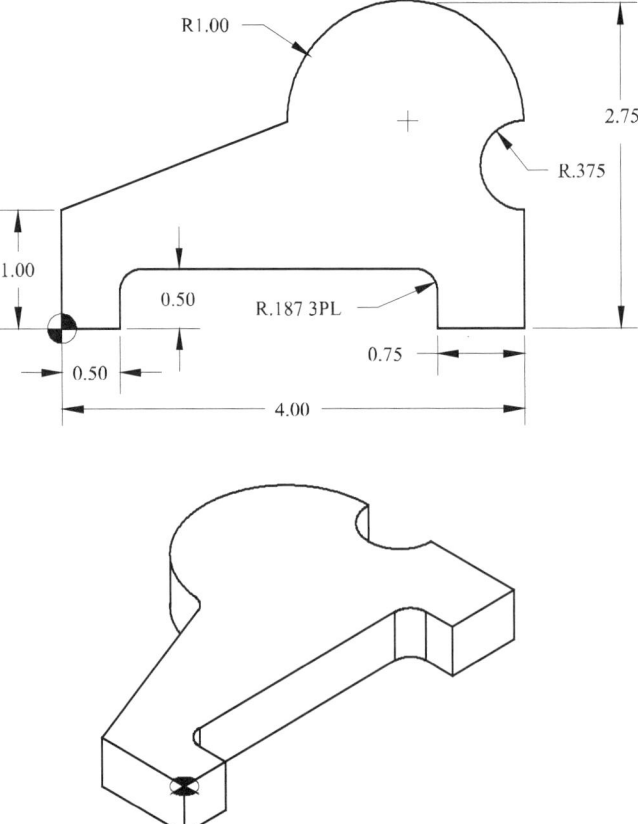

Figure 43 Machining Center Programming Exercise 5

Circle Milling

CNC Machining Center Exercise #6

Using G01, G02, or G03, program the moves required to mill the circular contour of this part. To enable cutting the entire step in one axial pass, you will need to make a calculation to select the correct minimum diameter end mill. Use climb mill directional cutting. The material is Carbon Steel and a hole of .500 inch diameter exists through the center of the part prior to this machining operation. The step depth is .375 inch and the circular pocket depth is .500 inch.

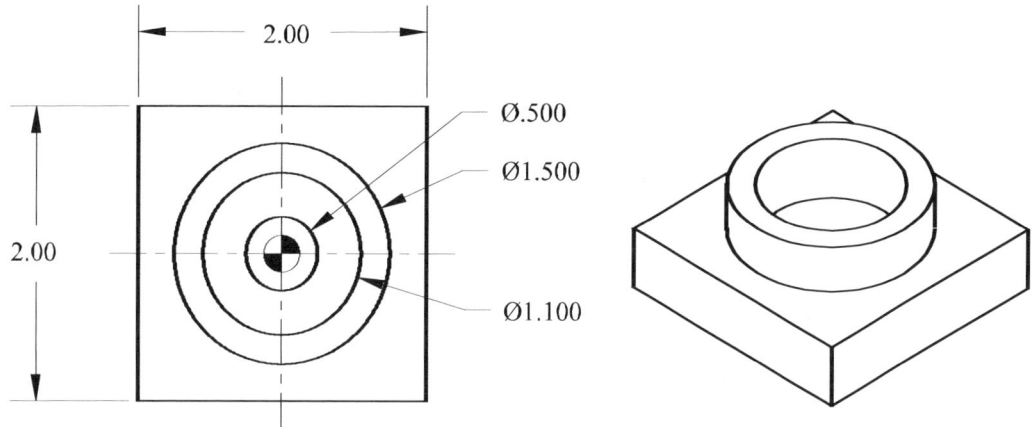

Figure 44 Machining Center Programming Exercise 6

Cutter Diameter Compensation

Using G01, G02, or G03 along with G41, G42 and G40 for cutter diameter compensation, follow the original directions and program the tool path moves required for each of the last four contour milling exercises.

CNC Machining Center Exercise #7

Cutter Diameter Compensation for Exercise 3

CNC Machining Center Exercise #8

Cutter Diameter Compensation for Exercise 4

CNC Machining Center Exercise #9

Cutter Diameter Compensation for Exercise 5

CNC Machining Center Exercise #10

Cutter Diameter Compensation for Exercise 6

Canned Cycles

CNC Machining Center Exercise #11

G81 Drilling

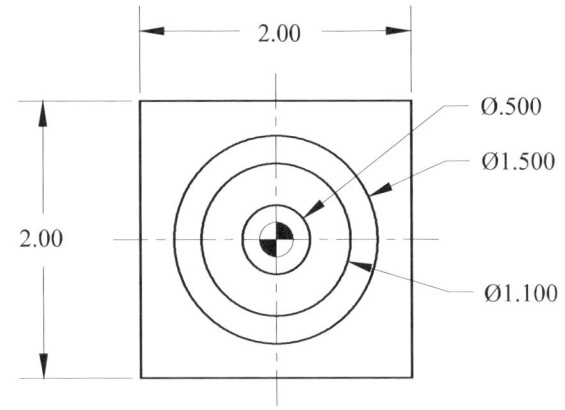

Figure 45
Machining Center Programming Exercise 11

In this exercise, you are required to center drill for and then drill a .500 inch hole at the origin of the part to 1/2 inch depth to the drill point. This activity should be added to the beginning of the prior Circle Milling exercise, before circle milling can begin, to aid in the entry of the end mill.

Figure 46
Machining Center Programming Exercise 12

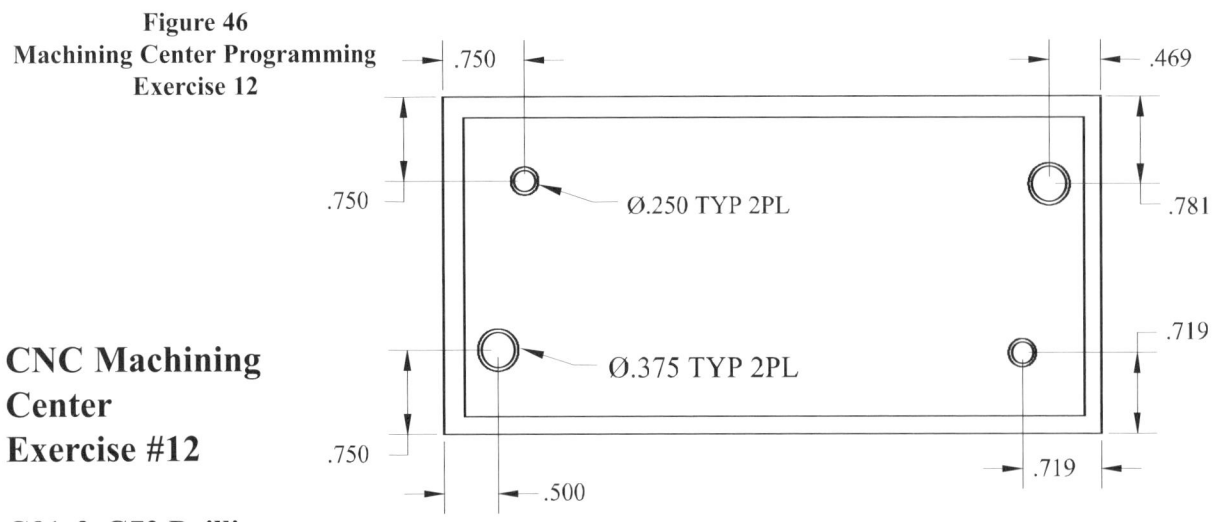

CNC Machining Center Exercise #12

G81 & G73 Drilling

In CNC Machining Center Exercise 3 above, you have programmed the milled step around the contour. In this exercise, you should add the holes to the existing program where required. They should be spot drilled deep enough to chamfer the top of the holes .015 inch, per side. Each of the holes are to be drilled through the material thickness of .750 inch.

CNC Machining Center Exercise #13

G81, G83 and G82 Drilling

In CNC Machining Center Exercise 4, you programmed the tool path for the milled step. In this example, you should add the counterbored holes to the existing program at .375 inch depth.

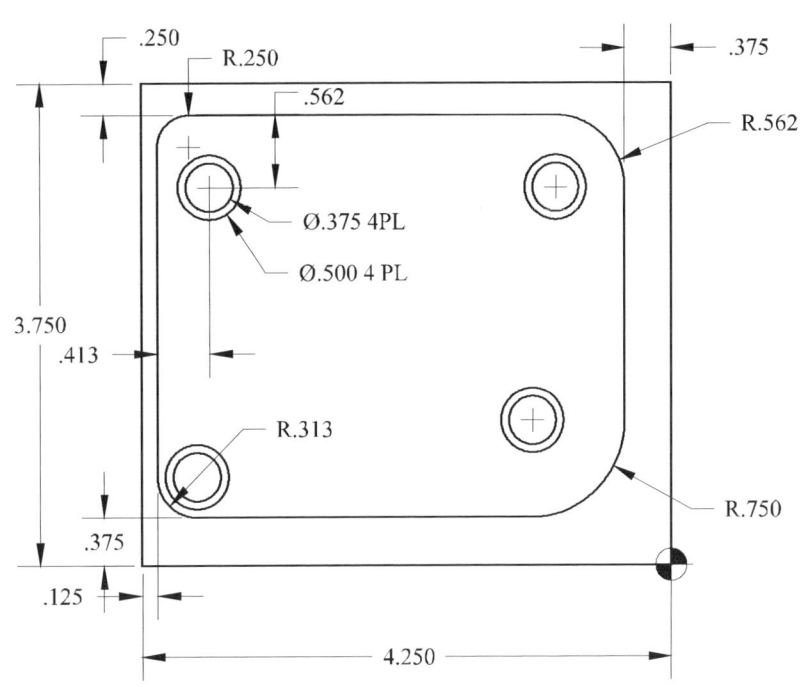

Figure 47
Machining Center Programming
Exercise 13

CNC Machining Center Exercise #14

G81, G83 Drilling and G84 Tapping

In this example, it is necessary to machine all of the holes in a plate that is 1.0 inch thick and is made of Aluminum. Use the G81, G82, G83 and G84 Canned Cycles to make the program. The part is already machined to the overall size and thickness dimensions. The maximum spindle r/min of the machine is 6000.

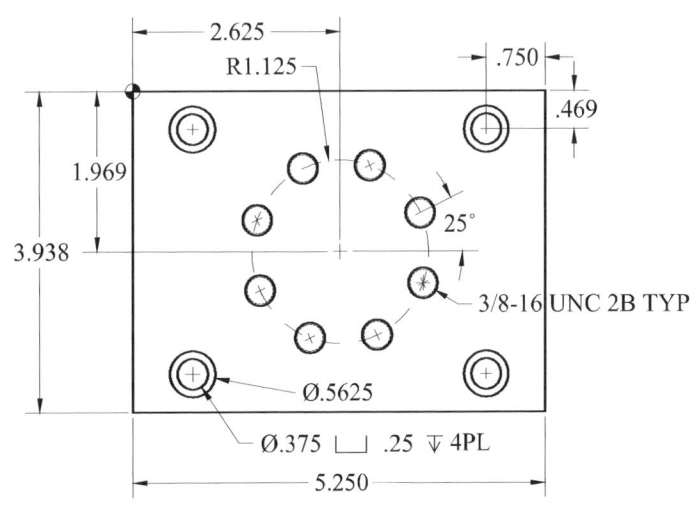

Figure 48
Machining Center Programming
Exercise 14

CNC Machining Center Combined Projects

CNC Machining Center Exercise #15

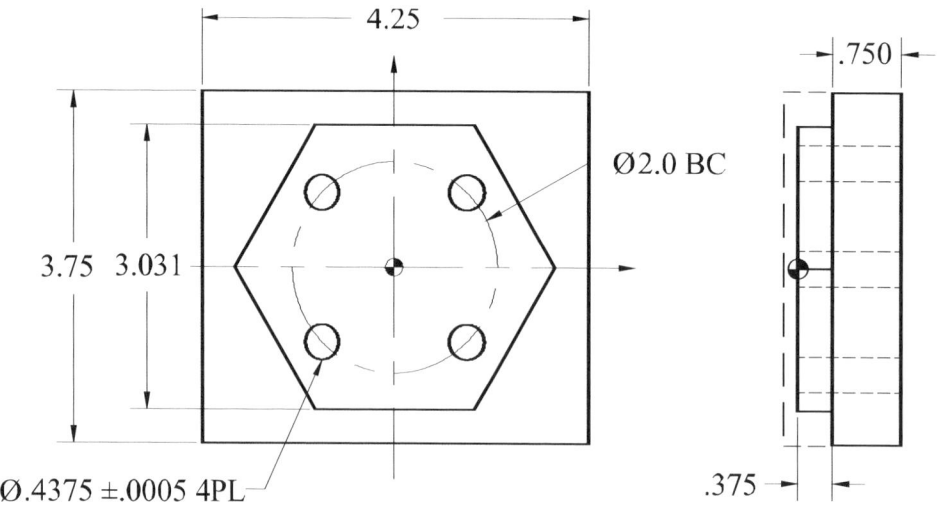

Figure 49 Machining Center Programming Exercise 15

In the Process Planning section of this workbook, you identified the operation, tools and setup information for the following part. Now use this information that you gathered to write a program for the same part. Note: the step may be axially roughed to within .030 inch with the face-mill and that the top surface must have .125 inch material removed, as well. In this case, the tool path should be programmed without the use of Cutter Radius Compensation (program the exact tool path) for the face mill.

CNC Machining Center Subprogram Application

M98 and M99 and G68

CNC Machining Center Exercise #16

In this project, there are several semicircular slots of the same size that need to be machined in the part. These are excellent candidates for subprogram application. Program one of the slots as a subprogram and call it multiple times from within the main program. Also, the use of coordinate system rotation (G68) will accommodate this. In this case, the part is aluminum and is 3/4 inch thick.

CNC Machining Center Exercise #17

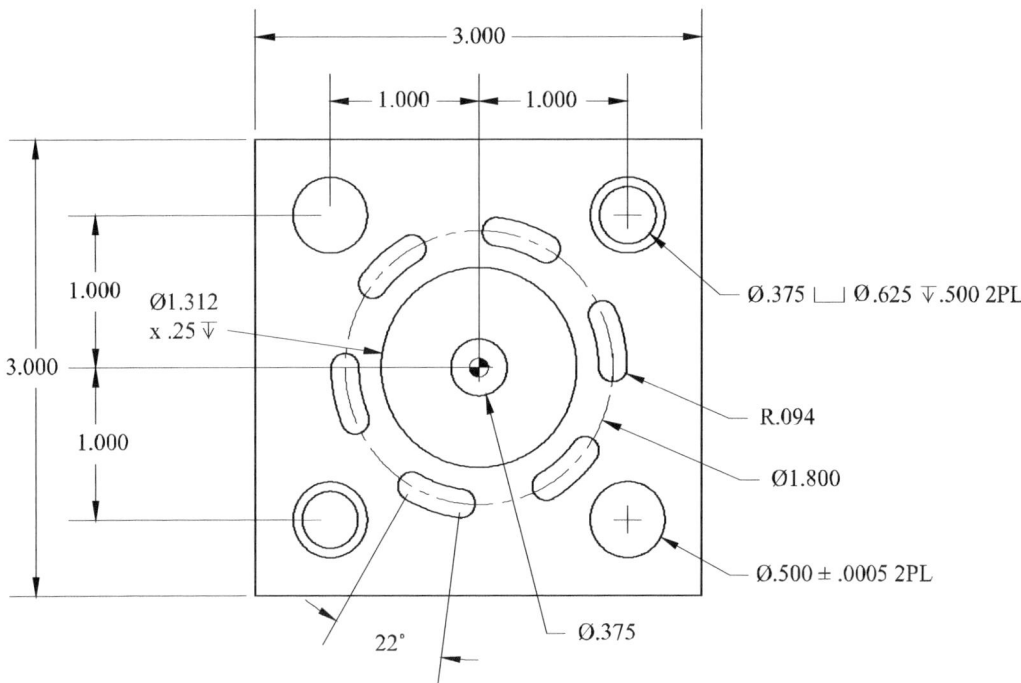

Figure 50 Machining Center Programming Exercise 16

In this example, it is necessary to machine all of the holes and step cutouts in the block in the drawing below (Figure 51). The material is Carbon Steel. Use the G98 command with Canned Cycles, where possible, to make the program. The part is already machined to the overall size and thickness dimensions.

CNC Machining Center Program Error Diagnosis

Use the skills you have learned to identify the problems in the following program lines and program sections. You may refer to the text, "Programming of CNC Machines" Third Edition.

1. Use the CNC code and sketch a representation of the part being created.

```
O3001
N100G90G17G20G80G49
(3/8 2 FLUTE  ENDMILL)
N105T1M6
N110G0G90G54X0.Y0.S1426M3
N108G43H1Z.1M8
```

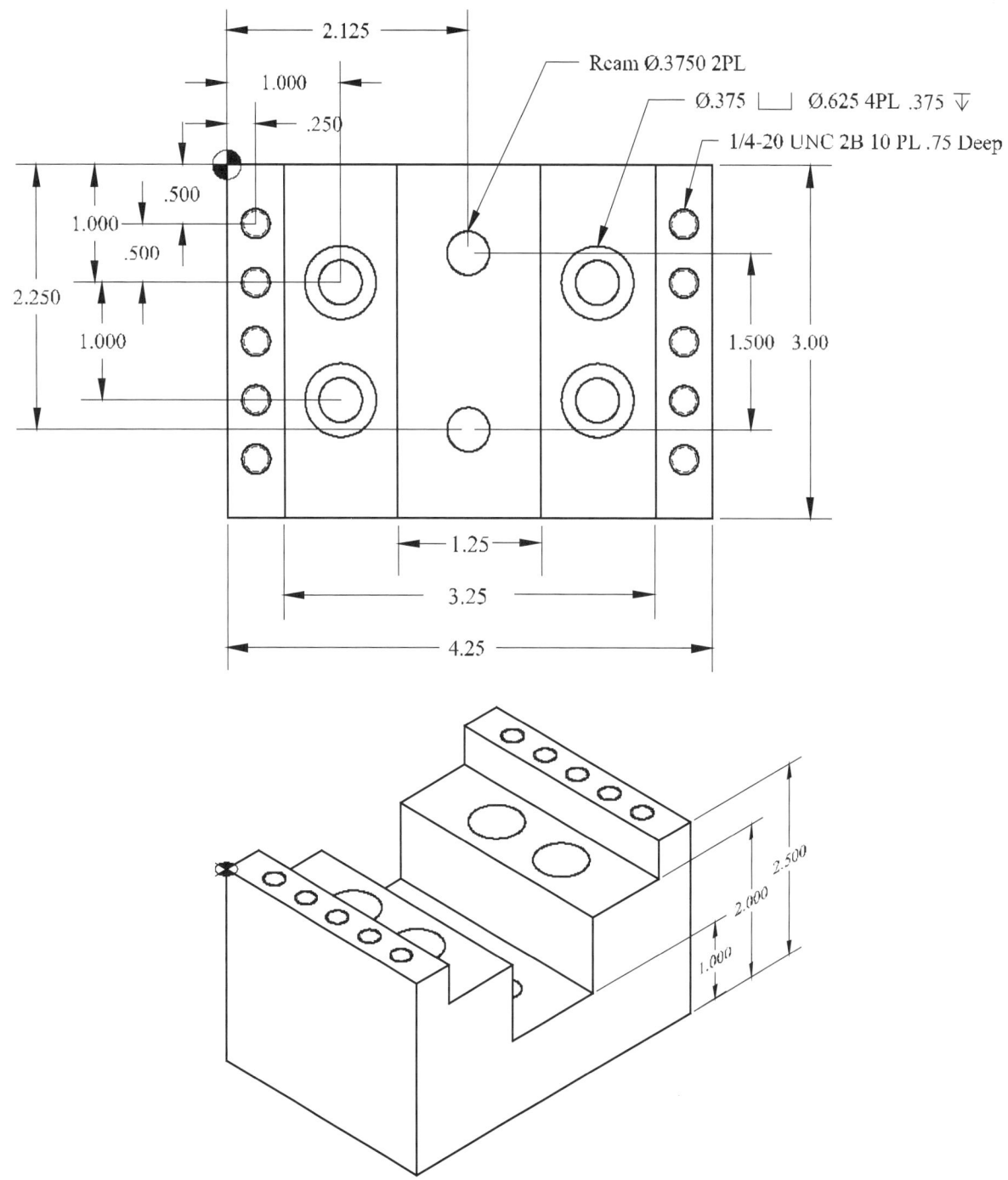

Figure 51 Machining Center Programming Exercise 17

N110G1Z-.1F6.33
N112G41D1Y6.
N114X1.Y7.
N116X1.5
N118X2.5Y6.
N120G3X4.5R1.
N122G1X11.Y2.5
N124Y1.
N126X10.Y0.
N128G40X0.
N130Z.1
N132M5
N134G91G0G28Z0.M9
N136G28X0.Y0.
N138M30

2. Identify the incorrect or missing information in the following program line.

N250G02X-.375Y2.938

3. Identify the incorrect or missing information in the following program line.

N110X-4.625F12.

4. Identify the incorrect or missing information in the following program line.

N25S2500M4

5. Identify the missing information in the following program line.

N125G83G99Z-1.13R.1F3.6

6. Identify the missing or incorrect information in the following program and/or subprogram.

O2010
N10G90G80G20G40G49M23
N15G00G54X-1.25Y.75S1000M03
N20G43Z1.0H01M08
N25G81G98Z-.35R.1F6.0
N30M98P7
N35G00G80X0

N40M21
N45G00X-1.25Y.75
N50G81G98Z-.35F6.R.1
N55M98P7
N60G00G80X0Y0
N65M23
N70M22
N75G00X-1.25Y.75
N80G81G98Z-.35F6.R.1
N85M98P7
N90G80G00X0Y0
N95M21
N100G00X-1.25Y.75
N105G81G98Z-.35F6.R.1
N110M98P7
N115G80Z1.0M09
N120M23
N125G91G28X0Y0Z0
N130M30

Subprogram for Program 2011

O2011	N5X-1.25
N1X-2.5	N6Y2.25
N2X-3.75	N7X-2.5
N3Y1.5	N8X-3.75
N4X-2.5	N9M30

7. Identify the missing information in the following program line.

N310G01G41X-4.125Y0

8. Identify the missing information in the following program line.

N10G90G20G80G49

9. Identify the missing information in the following program line.

N35G43Z1.0

ANSWER KEY
CNC BASICS ANSWERS

Process Planning Solutions

Turning Center Project

Review the following planning sheets for the Turning Center project and compare your answers.

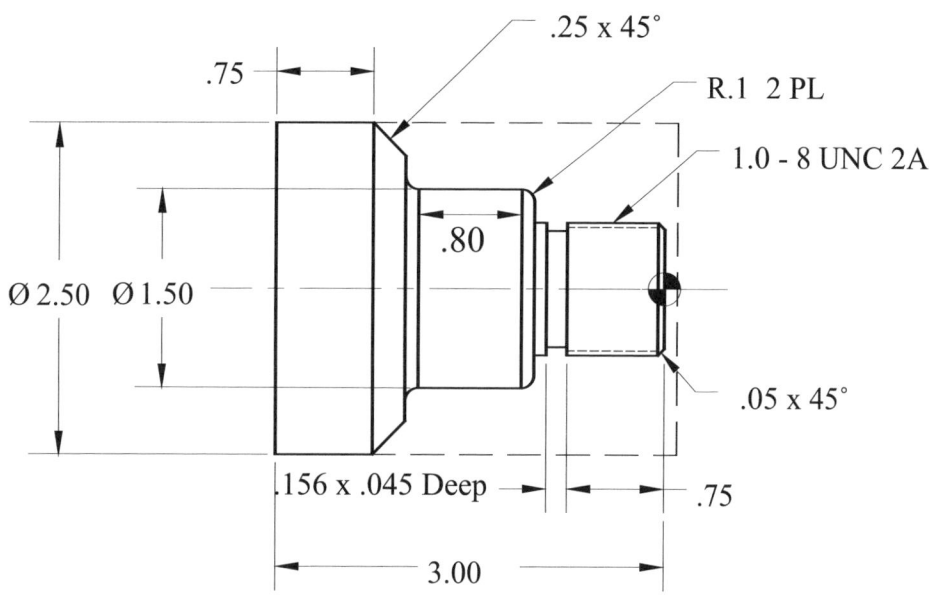

Figure 52
Turning Center Process Planning

Turning Center
Operation Sheet

Date:	Today	Prepared By:	You
Part Name:	Turning Center Project	Part Number:	1234
Quantity:	1	Sheet ___ of ___	
Material:	Alloy Steel		
Raw Stock Size:	3.0625" x 2.50" Diameter Bar Stock		

Operation Number	Machine Used	Description of Operation	Time
1	Saw	Cut the Bar Stock to 3.0625" lengths	
2	CNC Turning Center	Machine complete to dimensions	
3	Bench	Deburr as Needed	
4	QC	Final Quality Control Inspection	

Turning Center
CNC Setup Sheet

Date: Today	Prepared By: You
Part Name: Turning Center Project	Part Number: 1234
Machine: CNC Turning Center	Program Number:

Workpiece Zero: X = Centerline Y = NA Z = Finished Face

Setup Description:

Clamp the part in a 3-jaw chuck with soft-jaws, 2.35" minimum extended out of the chuck

Tool #	Tool Description	Offset #	Comments
1	Rough Turning Tool .031 TNRC	1	SFPM 125-1000
2	Finish Turning Tool .015 TNRC	2	SFPM 125-1000
5	O.D. Grooving Tool	5	.156 W ide .005 TNRC
7	O.D. Threading Tool	7	SFPM 125-1000

Facing Cut = r/min 191-1527
Turning 1.0 diameter, r/min = 477-3820
Turning 1.5 diameter, r/min = 318-2546
Turning 2.5 diameter, r/ min = 191-1528
Grooving .820 diameter, r/min = 582-4658
Threading r/min = 477-3820 Feed = Thread Lead

The preferred method of setting the r/min would be to use the Constant Cutting Speed (G96) command

Turning Center
Quality Control Check Sheet

Date: Today			Checked By:
Part Name: Turning Center Project		**Part Number:** 1234	
Blueprint Dimension	Tolerance	Actual Dimension	Comments
Ø 2.50	±.010		
Ø 1.50	±.010		
.75	±.010		
.25	±.010		
45°	±.5°		
R.1 2PL	±.015		
1.0 - 8 Thread	.9980/.9830		
1.0 - 8 Thread Pitch Ø	.9168/.9100		
.05	±.010		
45°	±.5°		
.75	±.010		
.156	±.005		
.09	±.010		
3.00	±.010		

Machining Center Project

Review the following planning sheets for the Machining Center project and compare your answers.

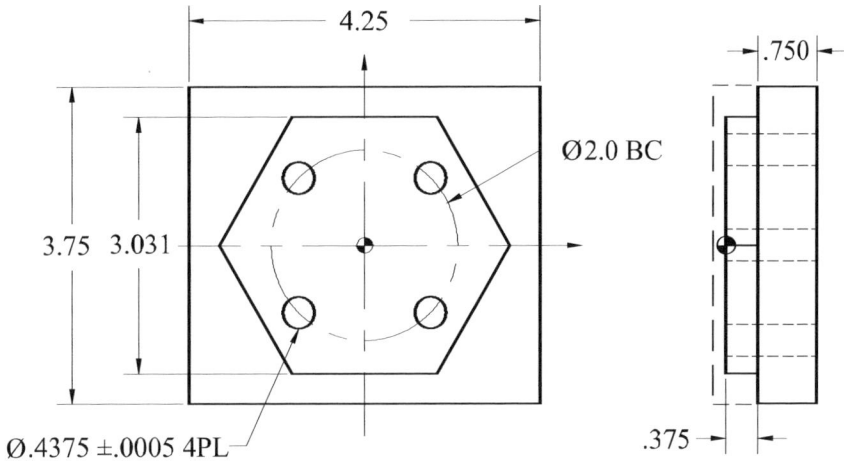

Figure 53 Machining Center Process Planning

Machining Center
Operation Sheet

Date:	Today	Prepared By:	You
Part Name:	Machining Center Project	Part Number:	1235
Quantity:	1	Sheet ___ of ___	
Material:	Aluminum		
Raw Stock Size:	4.5" x 1.25" Bar Stock		

Operation Number	Machine Used	Description of Operation	Time
1	Saw	Cut the Bar Stock to 3.875" lengths	
2	Mill	Machine Blanks to 4.25" x 3.75" finished size	
3	CNC Machining Center	Machine complete to dimensions	
4	Bench	Deburr as Needed	
5	QC	Final Quality Control Inspection	

Machining Center
CNC Setup Sheet

Date: Today	Prepared By: You
Part Name: Machining Center Project	Part Number: 1235
Machine: Machining Center	Program Number:

Workpiece Zero: X = Centerline Y =Centerline Z Top Most Finished Surface

Setup Description:

Clamp the part in a vise on parallels.
A minimum of 1/2" must be above the vise jaws.

Tool #	Tool Description	Offset #	Comments
1	3.0" Ø 5 Tooth Face Mill	1	SFPM 755-1720 in/tooth = .020-.039
2	.750" Ø 2 Flute End Mill	2	SFPM 165-850 in/tooth = .002-.006
3	.50" Ø x 90° Spotting Drill	3	SFPM 165-850 in/tooth = .002-.006
4	.4219" Ø 27/64 Drill	4	SFPM 165-850 in/tooth = .002-.006
5	.4375" Ø Reamer	5	r/min = 1/3 of lowest drill speed
			feed = 1/2 of lowest drill feed

Tool 1 = r/min 961-2190 = ipm 96.1-427.0
Tool 2 = r/min 840-4329 = ipm 17.32-51.9
Tool 3 = r/min 1260-6494 = ipm 2.52-38.96
Tool 4 = r/min 1494-7696 = ipm 5.98-92.35

Machining Center
Quality Control Check Sheet

Date: Today			Checked By:
Part Name: Machining Center Project		Part Number: 1235	
Blueprint Dimension	Tolerance	Actual Dimension	Comments
4.25	±.010		
Ø 3.0 BC	±.015		
Ø.4375	±.0005		
Ø.4375	±.0005		
Ø.4375	±.0005		
Ø.4375	±.0005		
3.75	±.010		
3.031	±.010		
3.031	±.010		
3.031	±.010		
.375	±.005		
.750	±.005		

Feeds and Speeds Answers

1. Alloy Steel SFPM = 125-1000
   r/min (RPM) = at the largest diameter (2.5) and the slowest CS, the r/min = 191
   and 1527 at the largest diameter and highest CS.
   in/rev =.008-.036
   D = 2.5 to 0

   Since the diameter reaches zero eventually, in facing, the r/min must change as the diameter changes. On a CNC lathe, the use of Constant Surface Speed is recommended G96 code. To accomplish a uniform SFPM, the r/min attained is limited by the max RPM of the Machine Tool.
   Depth of cut = since the amount of material to be removed is only 1/32, it would be the acceptable amount to use for a depth of cut. Depending on the surface finish requirement, it may also be acceptable to take 2 cuts at .0156 each.
   (See "Programming of CNC Machines", Part 3, Programming CNC Turning Centers, Constant Cutting Speed.)

2. Aluminum SFPM = 2800-4500
   r/min = 4625-7433
   Feed or in/rev = .017-.036

3. Carbon Steel SFPM = 30-160 for HSS tool
   r/min = 115-611

4. See the Turning Center project CNC Setup sheet above and compare your answers.

5. See the Machining Center project CNC Setup sheet above and compare your answers.

6. Stainless Steel SFPM = 20-80
   r/min = 142-569
   in/tooth .001-.003
   in/min = .284-3.4

7. Carbon Steel SFPM = 25-140
   Drill r/min = 80-448 and in/min = .160-3.58
   End Mill r/min = 114-640 and in/min = .456-10.24

8. Alloy Steel SFPM = 39-475
      r/min = 52-633
      in/tooth = .020-.039
      in/min = 5.2-123.43

9. Aluminum SFPM = 165-850 for an HSS cutter
      r/min = 1508-7770
      in/tooth = .002-..006
      in/min = 6.03-93.24

10.Check your answers with the speeds and feeds listed before each of the programs.

Coordinate Systems Answers

1. Absolute coordinates for each axis and for each point of the profile of the turned part, based on diametrical considerations.
X.90Z0, X1.0Z-.05, X1.0Z-.75, X.91Z-.75, X.82Z-.906, X1.0Z-.906, X1.0Z-1.0, X1.3Z-1.0, X1.5Z-1.1, X1.5Z-1.9, X1.7Z-2.0, X2.0Z-2.0, X2.5Z-2.25, X2.5Z-3.0

2. Incremental coordinates for each axis and for each point of the profile of the turned part, based on radial considerations.
X0Z0, X.450Z0, X.05Z-.05, X0Z-.70, X-.045Z0, X0Z-.156, X.09Z0, X0Z-.094, X.15Z0, X.1Z-.1, X0Z-.8, X.1Z-.1, X.25Z0, X.25Z-.25, X0Z-.75

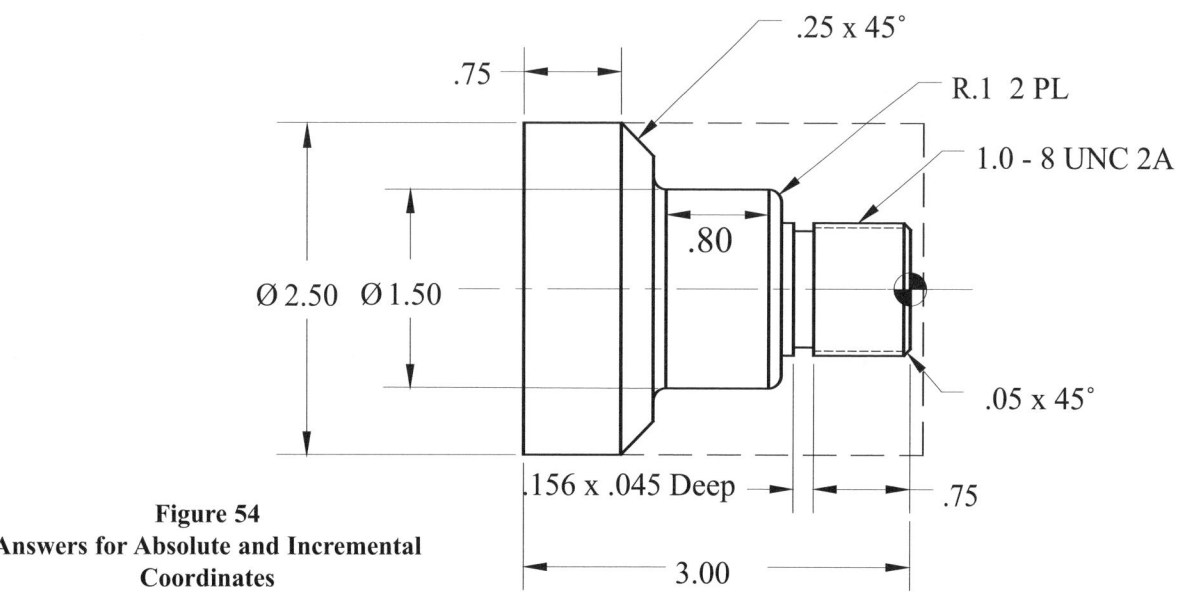

Figure 54
Answers for Absolute and Incremental
Coordinates

3. Absolute coordinates for each axis and for each point of the profile of the milled part. Start at part zero and proceed clockwise.
X0Y0, X0Y6.0, X1.0Y7.0, X1.5Y7.0, X2.5Y6, X4.5Y6, X11.0Y2.5, X11Y1.0, X10Y0

4. Incremental coordinates for each axis and for each point of the profile of the milled part.
X0Y0, X0Y6.0, X1.0Y1.0, X.5Y0, X1.0Y-1.0, X2Y0, X5.5Y-3.5, X0Y-1.5, X-1.0Y-1.0, X-10Y0

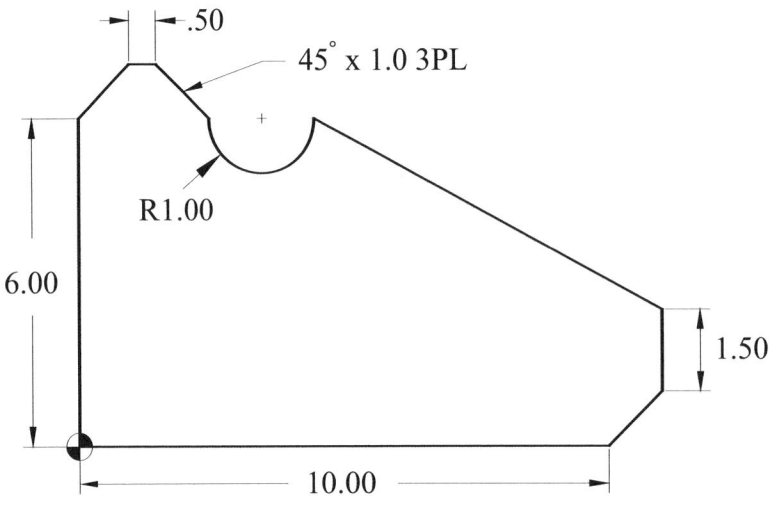

Figure 55 Answers for Absolute and Incremental Coordinates

5. Absolute coordinate values for X, Y and Z for each of the 15 points as indicated on the following drawing.
   1. X0Y0Z0, 2. X0Y-.75Z0, 3. X0Y-.75Z-.375, 4. X0Y-1.25Z-.375, 5. X0Y-1.25Z0,
   6. X0Y-2.0Z0, 7. X-3.0Y-2.0Z0, 8. X-3.0Y-1.25Z0, 9. X-3.0Y-1.25Z-.375, 10. X-3.0Y-.75Z-.375, 11. X-3.0Y-.75Z0, 12. X-3.0Y0Z0, 13. X-3.0Y0Z-2.25, 14. X-3.0Y-2.0Z-2.25, 15. X0Y-2.0Z-2.25

Figure 56
Answers for Absolute Coordinates

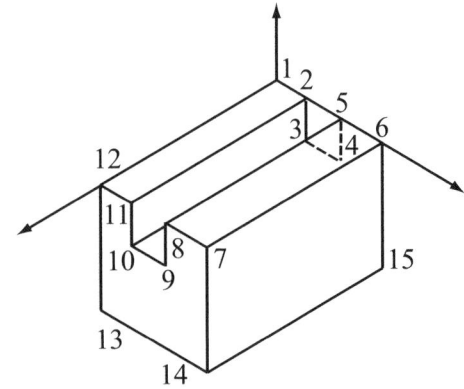

6. Identify each axis (vertical milling representation) and its positive or negative value on the following drawing:

7. Indicate the negative rotation direction for the polar coordinate system on the following drawing:

8. Indicate each of the polar quadrants on the following drawing:

9. Identify the angular value locations for 0, 90, 180, and 270 degrees on the following drawing:

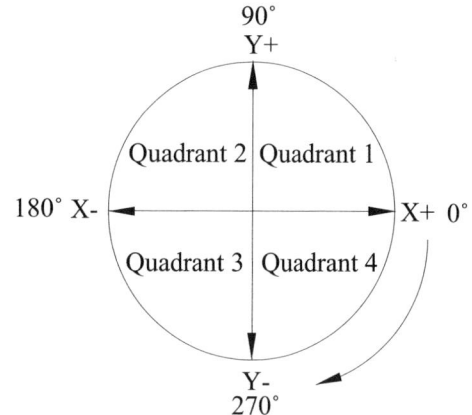

Figure 57 Answer for Vertical Milling Axes, Polar Rotation, Quadrants and Angular Values

10. Identify the polar (angular and radial) values for each of the holes on the following drawing:

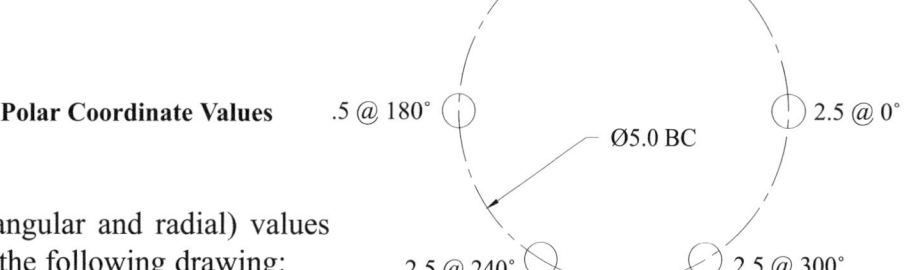

Figure 58 Answer for Polar Coordinate Values

11. Identify the polar (angular and radial) values for each of the holes on the following drawing:

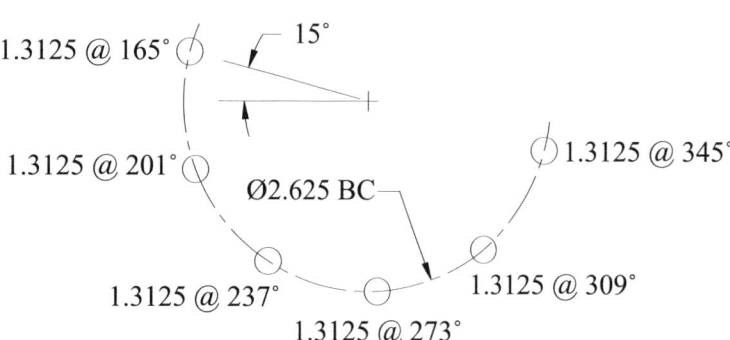

Figure 59 Answer for Polar Coordinate Values

Trigonometric Calculations Answers

1. Absolute rectangular coordinate locations for each hole center point.

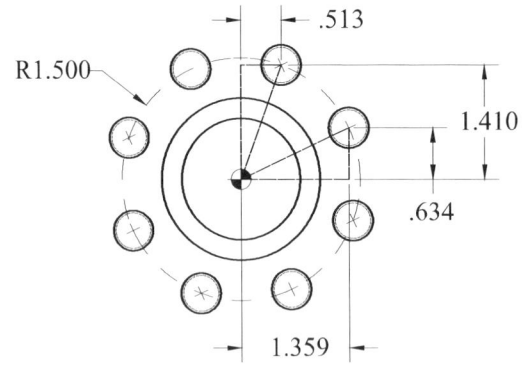

Figure 60
Answers for Calculate Absolute
Coordinates

X.513Y1.410, X1.359Y.634, X1.359Y-.634, X.513Y-1.410, X-.513Y-1.410, X-1.359Y -.634, X-1.359Y.634, X-.513Y1.410

2. Center-to-center dimension.
Use the Pythagorean theorem formula to calculate.

Figure 61
Answer for Calculate Center to Center Distance

3. Value for the unknown chord distance.
Use the Pythagorean Theorem formula to calculate.

Figure 62 Answer for Calculate Center to Center Distance

4. Values for each chord distance.
Using the Oblique triangle formulas and the values for a known side length and a known angle, calculate the chord values.

Figure 63
Answers for Calculate Chord Distance

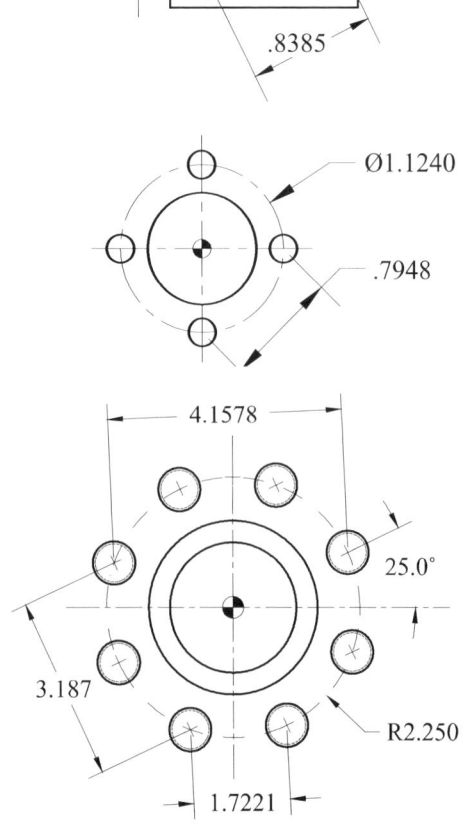

5. Tool travel necessary, to allow for the drill point.
.437/2 = .2185
.2185 * TAN 31° = .1313
.562 + .1313 = .6933

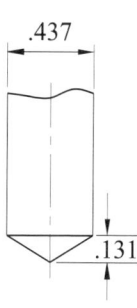

Figure 64
Answer for Calculate Drill Point Compensation

6. Depth of cut required to countersink to a diameter of .395 inch.

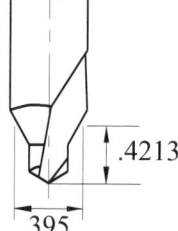

Figure 65
Answer for Calculate Drill Point Compensation

.0938 * TAN 30° = .054 (for the 120° tip)
The length from the 120° tip to the start of the 60° portion = .1875
.395 diameter - .1875 diameter/2 = .1038
.1038 * TAN 60° = .1798 (for the 60° portion)
.054 + .1798 + .1875 = .4213

7. Tool travel necessary, to allow for the drill point plus .090.
.090 + .875 + .0938 (drill point) = 1.0588

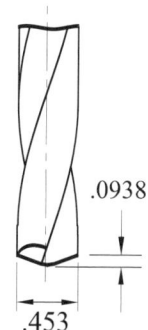

Figure 66
Answer for Calculate Drill Point Compensation

8. Offset amount for each axis and the coordinate values that will be required for the CNC program.

Figure 67
Answer for Calculate Cutter Offset Coordinates

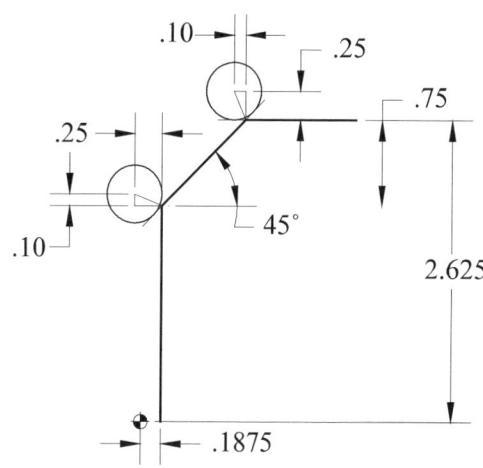

9. Offset for the tool nose radius when turning a 30°-tapered surface.

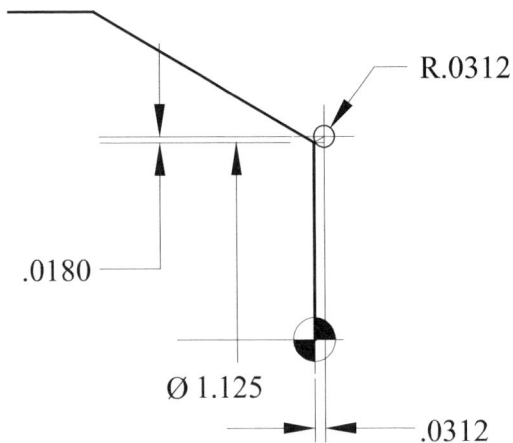

R.0312

Figure 68
Answer for Calculate Tool Nose Radius Offset
Coordinates

.0180

Ø 1.125

.0312

10. In the diagram below (Figure 69), a calculation is necessary to offset for the tool nose radius when turning a 30°-tapered surface. The face and centerline of the turned part are zero. List the coordinates needed in the CNC program, to allow for this offset.

11. Offset amount for the tool nose radius when turning a .062 inch 45° chamfer.

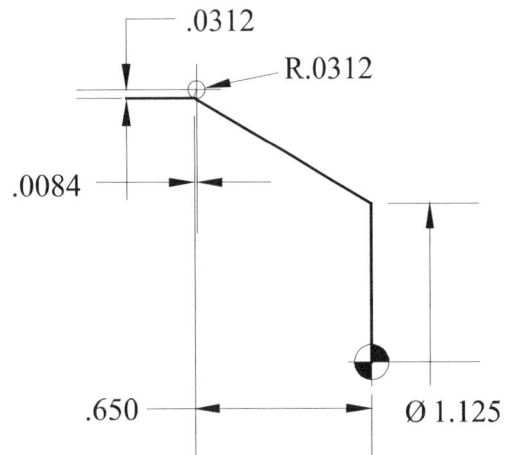

.0312

R.0312

.0084

.650   Ø 1.125

Figure 69
Answer for Calculate Tool Nose Radius Offset Coordinates

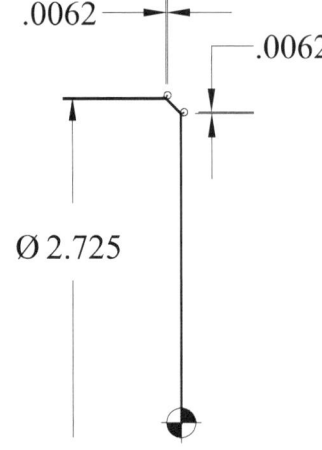

.0062

.0062

Ø 2.725

Figure 70
Answer for Calculate Tool Nose Radius

CNC Basics Study Question Answers

Answers are indicated in **BOLD** letters.

1. Programming is a method of defining tool movements through the application of numbers and corresponding coded letter symbols.

   T or F

2. A lathe has the following axes:
   a. X, Y & Z
   b. X & Y only
   c. X & Z only
   d. Y & Z only

3. Program coordinates that are based on a fixed origin are called:
   a. Incremental
   b. Absolute
   c. Relative
   d. Polar

4. On a two axis turning center the diameter controlling axis is:
   a. B
   b. A
   c. X
   d. Z

5. The letter addresses used to identify axes of rotation are:
   a. U, V & W
   b. X, Y & Z
   c. A, Z & X
   d. A, B & C

6. The acronym TLO stands for:
   a. Tool Length Offsets
   b. Total Length Offset
   c. Taper Length Offset
   d. Time Length Offset

7. When referring to the polar coordinate system, the clockwise rotation direction has a positive value.

   T or **F**

8. In Figure 15 of Part 1, CNC Basics, "Programming of CNC Machines", Third Edition, which quadrant is the part placed in?
   3

9. A program block is a single line of code followed by an end-of-block character.
   T or F

10. Each block contains one or more program words.
    T or F

11. Using Figure 13 in Part 1, CNC Basics, "Programming of CNC Machines", Third Edition,, list the X and Y absolute coordinates for the part profile where workpiece zero is at the lower left corner. (The corner cutoff is at a 45° angle).
    X0Y0, X0Y5.0, X2.5Y5.0, X4.0Y3.5, X4.0Y0, X0Y0

12. Using Figure 13 in Part 1, CNC Basics, "Programming of CNC Machines", Third Edition, list the X and Y incremental coordinates for the part profile where workpiece zero is at the lower left corner.
    X0Y0, X5.0Y2.5, X1.5Y-1.5, Y-3.5, X-4.0

13. How often should machine lubrication levels be checked?
    Daily

SETUP AND OPERATION ANSWERS

General Steps Answers

1. General steps required in preparing a CNC machine for production of a programmed part that has been effectively run before:
   Study the blueprint.
   Check the raw material requirements and verify compliance.
   Study any Planning Documents (i.e. Operation, CNC Setup and Quality Control sheets) supplied.
   Collect all required work holding and cutting tooling.
   Identify the program # and load it into the active controller memory.
   Install all work holding and cutting tools to their correct locations.
   Align (dial-in) work holding.
   Measure Tool Length Offsets (TLO).
   Measure Work Offset.
   Perform a tool path verification of the program on the control, where available.

Perform a dry run of the program cycle either without a part mounted or above the finished surface by some amount (commonly 1.0 inch), to physically verify machine movements and tool usage.

Remove any Z-axis offset used for the dry run procedure.

Set the rapid traverse to a reduced level.

Set the Optional Stop to an ON condition.

Use Single-Block operation for the first several moves to verify proper tool approach.

Automatic operation.

Perform in-process inspection at Program or Optional Stops and adjust where necessary.

Complete the program cycle.

Perform a 100% dimensional check of the part.

Production may begin after adjustments are made verified and a consecutive inspection is acceptable.

Operation Scenario Answers

2. Pulse Generator (Handle) magnitude increments.

X1 = a movement of .0001 inch or .0025 millimeters (mm)

X10 = a movement of .001 inch or .0254 mm

X100 = a movement of .010 inch or .254 mm

X1K = a movement of .100 inch or 2.54 mm

(See "Programming of CNC Machines" page 40-41 Part 2, Operation)

3. What will occur when the reset button is pressed during automatic operation? What steps should be followed to recover?

When the reset button is pressed during the automatic cycle, all feed movement will halt, spindle rotations will halt and coolant flow will halt. The program will be reset to the program beginning. In order to recover from this condition, the operator must switch to a manual mode (i.e. Jog or Handle), set the appropriate axis switch (commonly Z-axis), for removal of the tool that is in-cut, if necessary.

Move the tool to a clear position.

Home the machine or move it to a location where enough room is allowed to repair any problem that exists.

Replace or repair any broken tooling and re-measure the TLO.

Set the mode to EDIT and use the cursor or other search method to return the program to the beginning of its sequence for the tool in use, or press the reset button to set the program at its beginning, if applicable.

Return to the Automatic Operation mode and press cycle start. The rapid traverse override may be set to a lower level and the Single Block mode activated to ensure that proper positioning is attained.

4. What differences would exist when the Emergency Stop button is pressed during automatic operation, rather than the reset button and what will occur? What steps should be followed to recover?

       All of the same results will occur. The difference will be in the recovery. First a release of the E-Stop button will be required. Do so by twisting it in the clockwise direction until it pops back out. On some older machines (check the Operation Manuals supplied with the machine), it is required that the machine be "Homed" prior to returning to automatic operation. The other steps are identical as with the reset button condition.

5. When the Feed Hold button is pressed during automatic operation, what will occur? What steps should be followed to recover?

       When the Feed Hold button is pressed, only feed movement is stopped. The Spindle remains ON and coolant flow is not interrupted. Merely press the Cycle Start button again to resume automatic operation.

6. What mode of operation is required to install a tool into the spindle by the Automatic Tool Changer (ATC)?
   a. Automatic
   b. Jog
   c. Edit
   d. **Manual Data Input (MDI)**

7. What is the appropriate and safe method for performing in-process inspection measurements?

       If a program stop (M00) is in the program before each tool change, measurements can be taken at this time.

       If an optional stop (M01) is in the program before each tool change and the Optional Stop button is activated, measurements can be taken at this time.

       Another less popular method is to wait until the program is completed, and then measurements can be taken before the part is removed from the work holding device.

8. Where and how is the change made to compensate for a .003 inch diametrical variation for tool #4?

       To make the adjustment on the offset page, position the cursor under the wear column for tool offset #4 and input an amount of minus .003 inch. Press INPUT key.

9. Clearing of an existing wear offset for tool #4.

       Position the cursor to the tool #4's wear offset and use the numeric keypad to enter a value of zero, and then press the INPUT button. Or, position the cursor to tool #4's wear offset and use the numeric keypad to enter a value that is opposite the value shown (i.e. if the value is .003, then key in -.003) and press the INPUT+ button.

Restarting the program from a specific tool # from that point on.

In the EDIT mode, use the word search method to search to a specific word in the program, (i.e. T6) and follow these directions:

From the EDIT mode, use the alphanumeric keypad key in the letter address T.

Press the number 6.

Press the SRH soft key forward or reverse for the direction needed.

The cursor will move to the identified word T6.

Re-enter the automatic execution mode and press Cycle Start.

MDI Usage Answers

11. Several tasks that can be accomplished by using Manual Data Input MDI.

Turning the spindle ON, in a clockwise direction, at r/min. For the mill the code is S1000M3 and for the lathe G97S500M3.

Executing a tool change, for the mill, T1M6 and for the lathe T0101.

Turning ON the flood coolant flow, M08.

Turning OFF the coolant flow, M09.

Other common tasks that can be performed are:

The use of absolute rapid positioning moves that are based on a specific work offset, for example, G90G54G00X0Y0.

The execution of a tool offset to verify proper tool length measurement accuracy.

Use G43Z1.0H01 for milling or T0101Z.1 for turning.

Homing the machine by using the reference return command for milling G91G28Z0 and G28X0Y0 or for turning G28U0W0.

The execution of incremental feed moves for cutting vise jaws, etc. G91G01X-10.0F20.0.

Any command that can be a part of the program can be input and executed by using MDI. However, there is a limit of 10 lines of consecutive input in this mode. (See the text, "Programming of CNC Machines" Third Edition Part 2, CNC Machine Operation.

Programming Editing Answers

12. Altering of a program word G55 to G54 in an existing program.

From the EDIT mode, use a searching method to scan the program to the word to be altered.

Use the alphanumeric keypad to key the new address and the new data to be inserted.

Press the ALTER key.

The new data are changed.

To change the program word G55 in the example to G54, follow these steps:

Press the EDIT key.

Press the PRGRM soft key.

Key in the program word, G55.

Press the SRH soft key in the forward direction.

Key in the new program word, to insert, G54.

Press ALTER.

This procedure must be repeated to ensure that all instances of the incorrect offset calls are corrected. When using an offline editing software, a common method for doing this is called "find and replace".

13. Insertion of a missing program word into an existing program.

From the EDIT mode, use a searching method to scan the program to the word immediately before the word to be inserted.

Use the alphanumeric keypad to key the address and the data to be inserted.

Press the INSERT key.

The new data is inserted.

Example: To insert the program word T0101 on sequence number N15 of the program listed below:

Press the EDIT key

Press the PRGRM soft key

Key in the program word, S1000

Press the SRH soft key in the forward direction

Key in the new word, to insert, N2T0101

Press INSERT.

O1234

N10G50S1000

N20G96S600M03

N25G00X1.2Z.2

14. Deleting a program word from an existing program.

From the EDIT mode, use a searching method to scan the program to the word that needs to be deleted.

Then press the DELETE key.

To delete the program word (Date 03/29/07) from the example, follow these steps:

Press the EDIT key

Press the PRGRM soft key

Key in the word (Date 03/29/07)

Press the SRH soft key in the forward direction

Press DELETE.

Setup and Operation Study Question Answers

1. The counterclockwise direction of rotation is always a negative axis movement when referring to the handle/pulse generator.
    T or F

2. Which display includes the programmed Distance-to-Go readouts?
    Program Check

3. When the machine is ON and the program check screen is displayed, there is a list group of G-Codes displayed. What does this indicate?
    Default codes that are active

4. Describe the difference between the Input and the +Input soft keys in the function.
    The Input key when used inputs a whole number
    The Input + key when used inputs an incremental amount

5. Which button is used to activate automatic operation of a CNC program?
    a. Emergency Stop
    b. Cycle Stop
    c. Cycle Start
    d. Auto

6. Which display lists the CNC program?
    a. Position page
    b. Offset page
    c. Program check
    d. Program page

7. When the machine is turned on for the first time, it must be sent to its home position.
    T or F

8. Which operation selection button allows for the execution of a single CNC command?
    a. Dry run
    b. Single block
    c. Block delete
    d. Optional stop

9. Which mode switch/button enables the operator to make changes to the program?
    a. Edit

      b. MDI
      c. Auto
      d. Jog

10. What does the acronym MDI stand for?
      Manual Data Input

11. Which display screen is used to enter tool information?
      Offset

12. If the Reset button is pressed during automatic operation; spindle rotations, feed and coolant will stop.
      T or F

13. During setup, the mode switch used to allow for manual movement of the machine axes is:
      a. Auto
      b. MDI
      c. Edit
      d. Jog

CNC TURNING CENTER PROGRAMMING ANSWERS

The answer programs given here are only one method of machining the parts shown in the drawings. There are many possibilities for getting the correct results. Where possible, tool path verification and simulation programs should be used to confirm program integrity. The student should also consult with their instructor for program verification and always proceed, with caution, when running a newly written program. In the following exercises where only one tool is required, a CNC Setup sheet is not necessary but the tool and setup information should be listed before your program code. Please use a CNC Setup sheet in all other cases for the sake of clarity.

Programming Coordinate Identification for Turning Answers

1. Absolute programming coordinates including arc center locations with X-axis radial values.

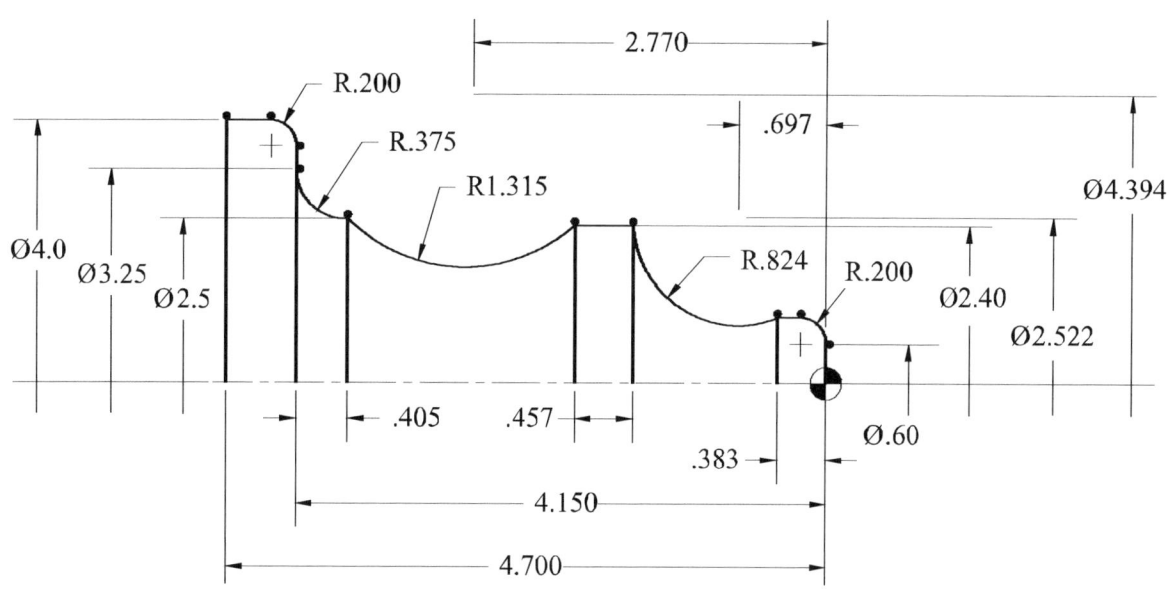

Figure 71 Answers for Identify Absolute and Incremental Coordinates

X0Z0, X.3Z0, (Arc Center = X.3Z-.2) X.5Z-.2, X.5Z-.383, (Arc Center = X1.261Z-.697) X1.2Z-1.521, X1.2Z-1.978, (Arc Center = X2.197Z-2.770) X1.25Z-3.745, (Arc Center = X1.625Z-3.775) X1.625Z-4.150, X1.80Z-4.150, (Arc Center = X1.80Z-4.35) X2.0Z-4.35, X2.0Z-4.7

Incremental programming coordinates including arc center locations with X-axis radial values.

X0Z0, U.3W0, (Arc Center = U0W-.2) U.2W-.2, U0W-.183, (Arc Center = U.761W-.314) U.7W-1.138, U0W-.457, (Arc Center = U.997W-.858), U.050W-1.767, (Arc Center = U.375W-

.030) U.375W-.405, U.175W0, (Arc Center = U0W-.2) U.2W-.2, U0W-.350

Linear Interpolation

Simple Turning Exercises

CNC Turning Center Programming Exercise 1 Program Code

Programmed tool path using linear interpolation (G01).

The dashed line on the drawing indicates the net shape of the part and the metal to be removed.

Caution: DO NOT attempt to execute this program from solid bar stock.

O0001
(CNC Turning Center Programming Exercise 1)
(Date, By)
(Tool #1, Rough Turning Tool)
N10T0100
N20G96S512M03
N30G00X2.35Z.1T0101M08
N40G1Z0F.0215
N50X-.01
N60Z.1
N70G0X.875
N80G1 Z-.700
N90X1.75
N100Z-1.455
N105X2.25
N110G0X2.35Z.1M09
N115G28U0W0
N120M30

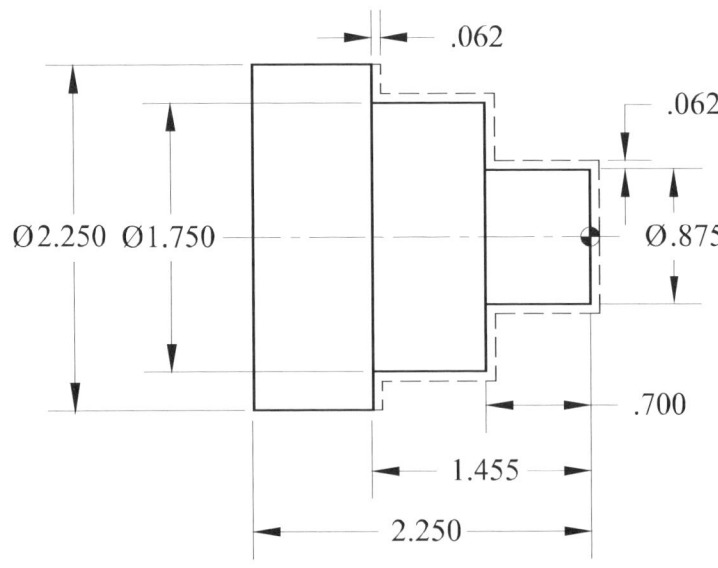

Figure 72
CNC Turning Center Programming Exercise 1

CNC Turning Center Programming Exercise 2 Program Code

Programmed tool path using linear interpolation (G01). The calculations necessary to offset the tool path for the Tool Nose Radius Compensation (TNRC) are given below. <u>The dashed line on the drawing indicates the net shape of the part and the metal to be removed.</u>

Caution: DO NOT attempt to execute this program from solid bar stock.

A calculation is required to determine the taper angle.

875 - .4375 = .4375
.4375/2 = .2188
A = ARCTAN .2188/.379
Angle A = 30°

A calculation is required to offset the tool path for the tool nose radius on the start of the tapered portion.

a = b * TAN 30°
.031 * .5774 = .0179
X axis value = .4375 + .0179 * 2 = .4733

A calculation is required to offset the tool path for the tool nose radius for the end of the tapered portion.

a = b * TAN 15°
.031 * .2679 = .0083
Z axis value = .379 - .0083 = .3707

A calculation is required to offset the tool path in the X-axis for the tool nose radius on the start of the first chamfer.

a = b * TAN 45°
.031 * 1.0 = .031
X axis value = 1.438 + .031 * 2 = 1.5

A calculation is required to offset the tool path in the Z-axis for the tool nose radius on the end of the first chamfer.

a = b * TAN 22.5°
.031 * .4142 = .0128
Z axis value = .856 - .0128 = .8432

A calculation is required to offset the tool path in the X-axis for the tool nose radius on the start of the second chamfer.

a = b * TAN 45°
.031 * 1.0 = .031
X axis value = 2.09 + .031 * 2 = 2.152

A calculation is required to offset the tool path in the Z-axis for the tool nose radius on the end of the second chamfer.

a = b * TAN 22.5°
.031 * .4142 = .0128
Z axis value = 1.455 - .0128 = 1.4422

Figure 73
CNC Turning Center
Programming Exercise 2

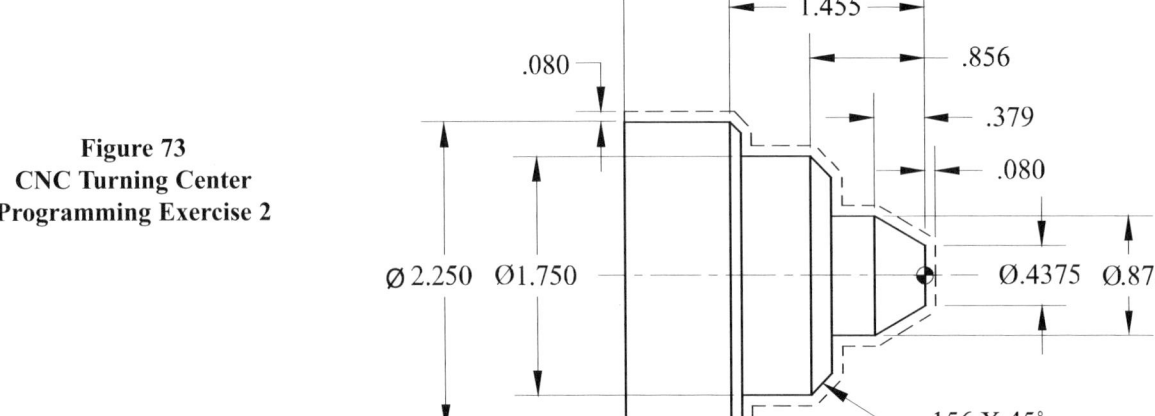

O0002
(CNC Turning Center Programming Exercise 2)
(Date, By)
(Tool #1, Rough Turning Tool)
N10T0100
N20G96S563M03
N30G00X.6975Z.1T0101M08
N40G1Z0F.022
N50X-.01
N60Z.1
N70G0X.4733
N80G1Z0
N90X.875Z-.3707
N100Z-.7
N110X1.5
N120X1.75Z-.8432
N130Z-1.375
N140X2.152
N150X2.25Z-1.4422

N160Z-2.25
N170G0X2.35Z.1M09
N180G28U0W0
N190M30

CNC Turning Center Programming Exercise 3 Program Code

Face using Fixed Cutting Cycle B (G94), in 3 equal depths of cut passes.

O0003
(CNC Turning Center Programming Exercise 3)
(Date, By)
(Tool #1, Rough Turning Tool)
N10T0100
N20G96S513M03
N30G00X1.85Z.1T0101M08
N40G94X-.03Z-.0623F.022
N50Z-.1247
N60Z-.187
N70G28U0W0M09
N80M30

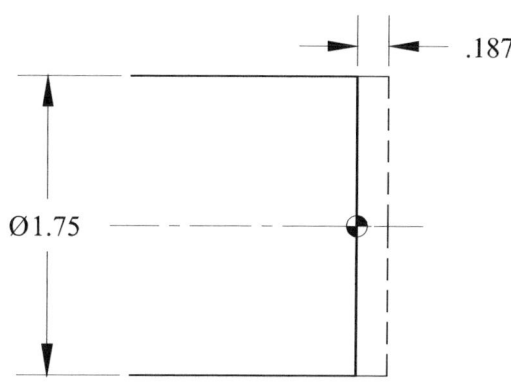

Figure 74
CNC Turning Center Programming Exercise 3

CNC Turning Center Programming Exercise 4 Program Code

Turn using Fixed Cutting Cycle A (G90), in 3 equal depths of cut passes.

O0004
(CNC Turning Center Programming Exercise 4)
(Date, By)
(Tool #1, Rough Turning Tool)
N10T0100
N20G96S513M03
N30G00X1.85Z.1T0101M08
N40G90X1.625Z-1.12F.022
N50X1.500
N60X1.375
N70G28U0W0M09
N80M30

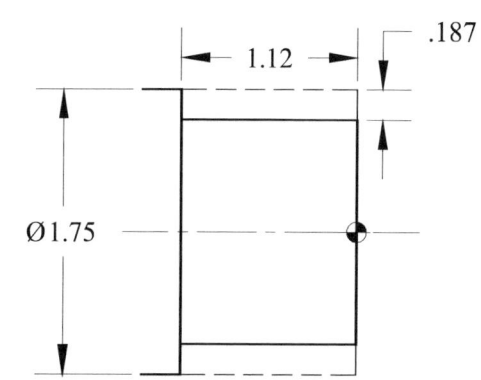

Figure 75
CNC Turning Center Programming Exercise 4

Linear and Circular Interpolation

CNC Turning Center Programming Exercise 5 Program Code

Programmed tool path using linear and circular interpolation (G01 and G03).
   The dashed line on the drawing indicates the net shape of the part and the metal to be removed.
   Caution: DO NOT attempt to execute this program from solid bar stock.

O0005
(CNC Turning Center Programming Exercise 5)
(Date, By)
(Tool #1, Rough Turning Tool)
N10T0100
N20G50S6000
N30G96S3650M03
N40G00X0Z.1T0101M08
N50G1Z0F.0265
N60X.125
N70G3X.875Z-.375R.406
N80G1Z-.7
N90X1.188
N100G3X1.75Z-.981R.312
N110G1Z-1.375
N120G3X2.25Z-1.656R.312
N130G1Z-2.25
N140G0X2.35Z.1M09
N150G28U0W0
N160M30

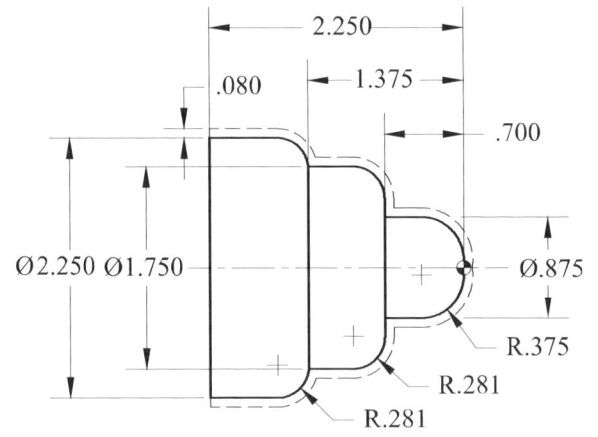

Figure 76
CNC Turning Center Programming Exercise 5

The following is the same program written using the I and K commands for the arcs.

O0005
(CNC Turning Center Programming Exercise 5)
(Date, By)
(Tool #1, Rough Turning Tool)
N10T0100
N20G50S6000
N30G96S3650M03

```
N40G00X0Z.1T0101M08
N50G1Z0F.0265
N60X.125
N70G3X.875Z-.375I.0K-.437
N80G1Z-.7
N90X1.188
N100G3X1.75Z-.981I0K-.343
N110G1Z-1.375
N120G3X2.25Z-1.656I0K-.374
N130G1Z-2.25
N140G0X2.35Z.1M09
N150G28U0W0
N160M30
```

CNC Turning Center Programming Exercise 6 Program Code

Programmed tool path using linear and circular interpolation (G01, G02 and G03).

<u>The dashed line on the drawing indicates the net shape of the part and the metal to be removed.</u>

Caution: DO NOT attempt to execute this program from solid bar stock.

```
O0006
(CNC Turning Center
Programming Exercise 6)
(Date, By)
(Tool #1, Rough Turning Tool)
N10T0100
N20G50S6000
N30G96S3650M03
N40G00X0Z.1T0101M08
N50G1Z0F.0265
N60G3X.715Z-.3575R.3885
N70G1Z-.655
N80G2X.965Z-.749R.094
N90G1X1.252
N100G3X1.626Z-.967R.218
N110G1Z-1.255
```

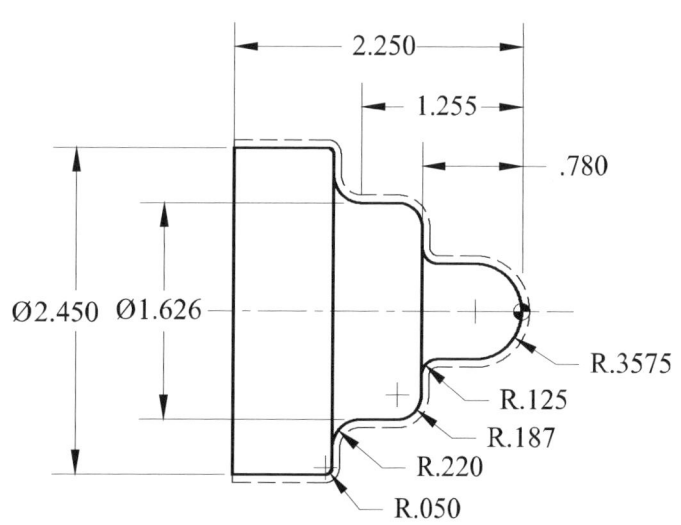

Figure 77
CNC Turning Center Programming Exercise 6

N120G2X2.066Z-1.475R.189

The following is the same program written using the I and K commands for the arcs.

O0006
(CNC Turning Center Programming Exercise 6)
(Date, By)
(Tool #1, Rough Turning Tool)
N10T0100
N20G50S6000
N30G96S3650M03
N40G00X0Z.1T0101M08
N50G1Z0F.0265
N60G3X.715Z-.3575I0K-.3885
N70G1Z-.655
N80G2X.965Z-.780I.094K0
N90G1X1.252
N100G3X1.626Z-.967I0K-.218
N110G1Z-1.255
N120G2X2.066Z-1.475I.189K0
N130G1X2.35
N140G3X2.45Z-1.525I0K-.081
N150G1Z-2.25
N160G0X2.55Z.1M09
N170G28U0W0
N180M30

Tool Nose Radius Compensation

Note: The correct values must be set in the offset register for each of the tools, identifying the amount of the tool nose radius compensation. Even if they are called properly in the program, the correct result will not occur if these values are not set properly. This method will differ, to some degree, dependant on the specific controller used. You should consult the Operation and Programming manuals specific to the machine and controller being used.

CNC Turning Center Programming Exercise 7 Program Code

Exercise 2 with TNRC

The following program is the tool path using linear and circular interpolation and TNRC (G40, G41 and G42). The dashed line on the drawing indicates the net shape of the part and the metal to be removed.

Caution: DO NOT attempt to execute this program from solid bar stock.

```
O0007
(CNC Turning Center Programming Exercise 7)
(Date, By)
(Tool #1, Rough Turning Tool)
N10T0100
N20G96S563M03
N30G00G41X.6975Z.1T0101M08
N40G1Z0F.022
N50X-.01
N60G0Z.1
N70G42X.4375
N80G1Z0
N90X.875Z-.379
N100Z-.7
N110X1.438
N120X1.75Z-.856
N130Z-1.375
N140X2.09
N150X2.25Z-1.455
N160Z-2.25
N170G0G40X2.35Z.1M09
N180G28U0W0
N190M30
```

CNC Turning Center Programming Exercise 8 Program Code

Exercise 5 with TNRC

The dashed line on the drawing indicates the net shape of the part and the metal to be removed.

Caution: DO NOT attempt to execute this program from solid bar stock.

O0008
(CNC Turning Center Programming Exercise 8)
(Date, By)
(Tool #1, Rough Turning Tool)
N10T0100
N20G50S6000
N30G96S3650M03
N40G00G42X0Z.1T0101M08
N50G1Z0F.0265
N60X.125
N70G3X.875Z-.375R.375
N80G1Z-.7
N90X1.188
N100G3X1.75Z-.981R.281
N110G1Z-1.375
N120G3X2.25Z-1.656R.281
N130G1Z-2.25
N140G0G40X2.35Z.1M09
N150G28U0W0
N160M30

The following is the same program written using the I and K commands for the arcs.
O0008
(CNC Turning Center Programming Exercise 8)
(Date, By)
(Tool #1, Rough Turning Tool)
N10T0100
N20G50S6000
N30G96S3650M03
N40G00G42X0Z.1T0101M08
N50G1Z0F.0265
N60X.125
N70G3X.875Z-.375I0K-.375
N80G1Z-.7
N90X1.188
N100G3X1.75Z-.981I0K-.281
N110G1Z-1.375
N120G3X2.25Z-1.656I0K-.281
N130G1Z-2.25
N140G0G40X2.35Z.1M09
N150G28U0W0
N160M30

CNC Turning Center Programming Exercise 9 Program Code

Exercise 6 with TNRC

The dashed line on the drawing indicates the net shape of the part and the metal to be removed.

Caution: DO NOT attempt to execute this program from solid bar stock.

```
O0009
(CNC Turning Center Programming Exercise 9)
(Date, By)
(Tool #1, Rough Turning Tool)
N10T0100
N20G50S6000
N30G96S3650M03
N40G00G42X0Z.1T0101M08
N50G1Z0F.0265
N60G3X.715Z-.3575R.3575
N70G1Z-.655
N80G2X.965Z-.780R.125
N90G1X1.252
N100G3X1.626Z-.967R.187
N110G1Z-1.255
N120G2X2.066Z-1.475R.22
N130G1X2.35
N140G3X2.45Z-1.525R.05
N150G1Z-2.25
N160G0G40X2.55Z.1M09
N170G28U0W0
N180M30
```

The following is the same program written using the I and K commands for the arcs.

```
O0009
(CNC Turning Center Programming Exercise 9)
(Date, By)
(Tool #1, Rough Turning Tool)
N10T0100
N20G50S6000
N30G96S3650M03
N40G00G42X0Z.1T0101M08
N50G1Z0F.0265
```

N60G3X.715Z-.3575I0K-.3575
N70G1Z-.655
N80G2X.965Z-.780I.125K0
N90G1X1.252
N100G3X1.626Z-.967I0K-.187
N110G1Z-1.255
N120G2X2.066Z-1.475I.22K0
N130G1X2.35
N140G3X2.45Z-1.525I0K-.05
N150G1Z-2.25
N160G0G40X2.55Z.1M09
N170G28U0W0
N180M30

Drilling

CNC Turning Center Programming Exercise 10 Program Code

Programmed tool path using linear interpolation (G01) to center drill.

Calculate the depth of cut required using a #5 (Plain Type) center drill to countersink to a diameter of .405 inch. Plain Type center drills have an angle of 60° with a point angle of 120°. The length from the end of the point angle to the beginning of the 60° angle is 3/16 inch (See *Machinery's Handbook,* page 844, 25th Edition).

.0938 * TAN 30° = .054 (for the 120° tip)
.109 * TAN 60° = .1888 (for the 60° portion)
.054 + .1888 + .1875 = .4303

O0010
(CNC Turning Center Programming Exercise 10)
(Date, By)
(Tool 9 = #5 Center Drill)
N10T0900
N20G97S641M03
N30G00X0Z.1T0909M08
N40G1Z-.4303F.009
N50G0Z.1M09
N60G28U0W0T0900
N70M30

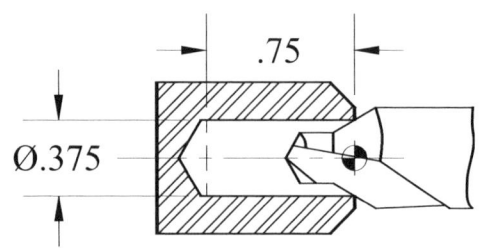

Figure 78
CNC Turning Center Programming Exercise 10

CNC Turning Center Programming Exercise 11 Program Code

G74

Programmed tool path using the drilling cycle G74 with 3 equal depth cuts.

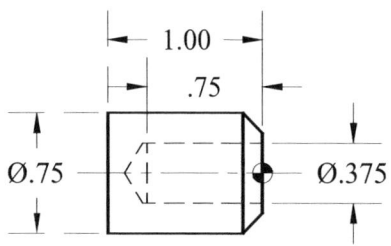

Figure 79
CNC Turning Center Programming
Exercise 11

```
O0011
(CNC Turning Center Programming Exercise 11)
(Date, By)
(Tool 9 = #5 Center Drill)
N10T0900
N20G97S641M03
N30G00X0Z.1T0909M08
N40G1Z-.4303F.009
N50G0Z.1M09
N60G28U0W0T0900
N70M01
(Tool 10 = .375 Diameter HSS Drill)
N80T1000
N90G97S693M03
N100G0X0Z.1T1010M08
N110G74R.1
N120G74X0Z-1.0Q.333F.009
N130G0Z.1M09
N140G28U0W0T0900
N150M30
```

Multiple Repetitive Cycles

CNC Turning Center Programming Exercise 12 Program Code

G71 & G70 Rough and Finish Turn cycle

Programmed tool path using Turning Cycles (G71 and G70).

O0012

(CNC Turning Center Programming Exercise 12)
(Date, By)
(Tool #1, Rough Turning Tool)
N10T0100
N20G50S6000
N30G96S2800M3
N40G0X3.1Z.1T0101M08
N50G1Z0F.0265
N60X-.01
N70G0Z.1
N80G42X3.0
N90G71U.08R.1
N100G71P110Q210U.015W.005
N110G0X.94
N115G01Z0F.0265
N120G3X1.0Z-.03R.03
N130Z-.94
N140G2X1.12Z-1.0R.06
N150G01X1.8
N160X2.0Z-1.1
N170Z-1.94
N180G2X2.12Z-2.0R.06
N190G01X2.8
N200X3.0Z-2.1
N210X3.1
N220G28G40U0W0T0100
N230M01
(Tool #2, Finish Turning Tool)
N240T0200
N250G50S6000
N260G96S2800M3
N270G0G42X3.1Z.1T0202M08
N280G70P110Q210
N290G28G40U0W0T0200M09
N300M30

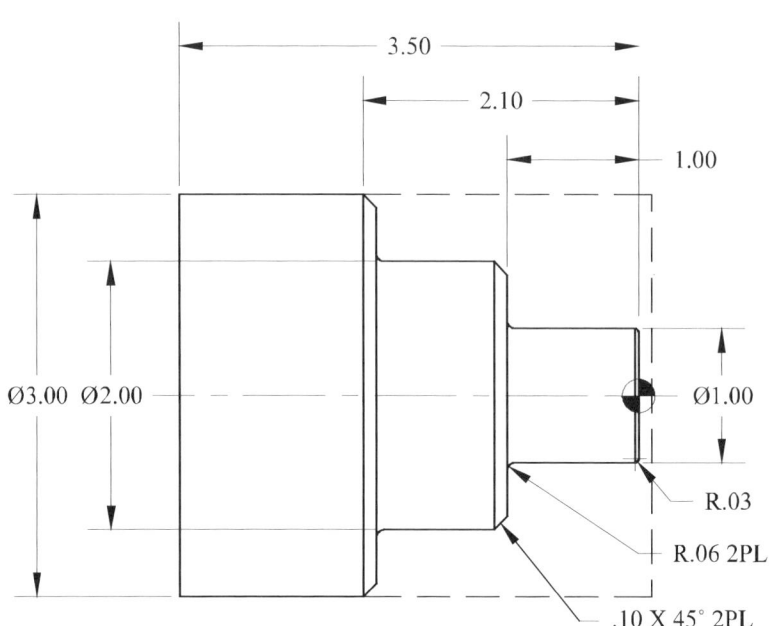

Figure 80
CNC Turning Center Programming Exercise 12

Note: To use the single block format for program #O0012, omit line N90 and replace line N100 with: N100G71P110Q210U.015W.005D.08

Boring

CNC Turning Center Programming Exercise 13 Program Code

G71 & G70 Rough and Finish Turn cycle

The same rough and Finish Turning Cycles (G71 and G70), applied to internal boring.

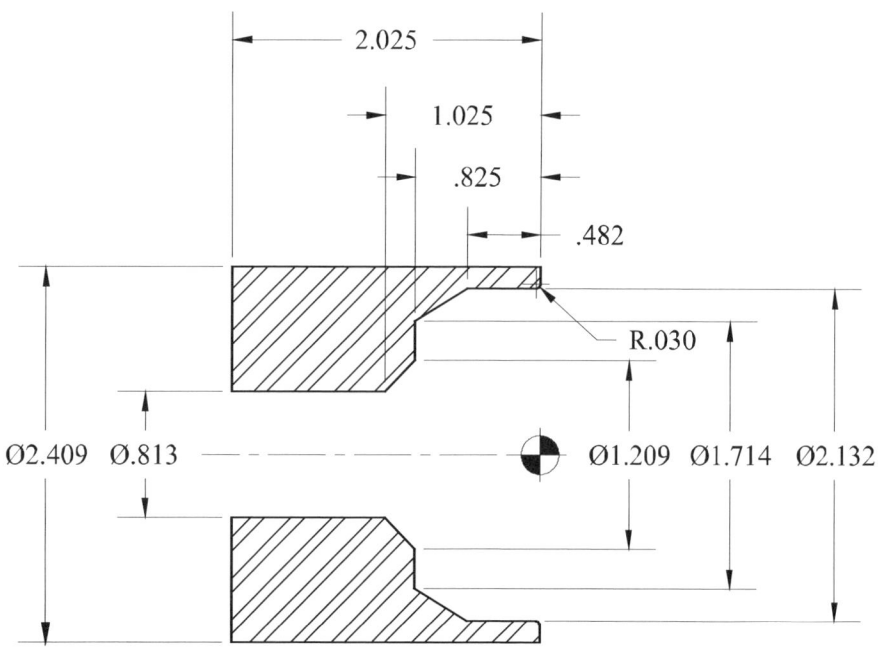

Figure 81 CNC Turning Center Programming Exercise 13

O0013
(CNC Turning Center Programming Exercise 13)
(Date, By)
(Tool #3, Rough Boring Tool)
N10T0300
N20G50S6000
N30G96S2800M3
N40G0X.713Z.1T0303M08
N50G71U.08R.03
N60G71P70Q140U.015W.005
N70G0X2.192
N80G01Z0F.0265
N90G2X2.132Z-.03R.03

N100G01Z-.482
N110X1.714Z-.825
N120X1.209
N130X.813Z-1.025
N140X.713
N150G28G40U0W0T0300
N160M01
(Tool #4, Finish Boring Tool)
N170T0400
N180G50S6000
N190G96S2800M3
N200G0G42X.90Z.1T0404M08
N210G70P80Q140
N220G28G40U0W0T0400M09
N230M30
Note: To use the single block format for program #O0013, omit line N50 and replace line N60 with: N60G71P70Q140U.015W.005D.08

CNC Turning Center Programming Exercise 14 Program Code

G72 Face Cutting Cycle

Programmed tool path using the Face Cutting Cycle (G72).

O0014
(CNC Turning Center Programming Exercise 14)
(Date, By)
(Tool #1, Rough Turning Tool)
N10T0100
N20G50S6000
N30G96S2800M3
N40G0G41X2.005Z.1T0101M08
N50G72U.06R.1
N60G72P70Q190U.015W.015
N70G0Z-.563
N80G1X1.905F.0265
N90Z-.523
N100G2X1.785Z-.463R.06
N110G1X1.305

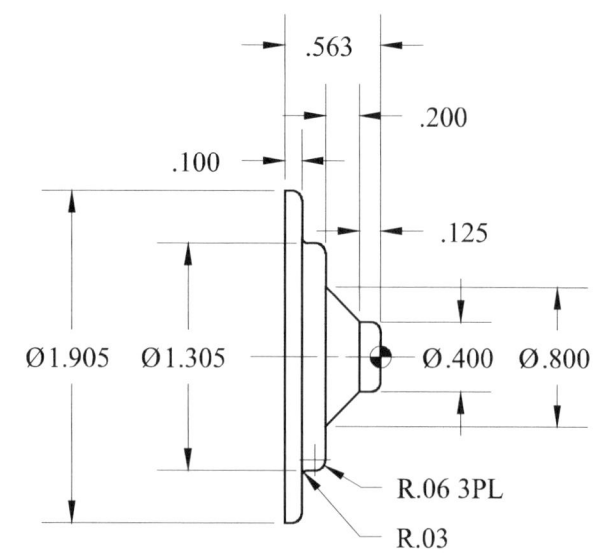

Figure 82
CNC Turning Center Programming Exercise 14

N120Z-.41
N130G2X1.185Z-.325R.06
N140G1X.8
N150X.4Z-.125
N160Z-.06
N170G2X.28Z0R.06
N180G1X0
N190G0G40Z.1
N200G28U0W0T0100
N210M01
(Tool #2, Finish Turning Tool)
N220T0200
N230G50S6000
N240G96S2800M3
N250G0G41X.90Z.1T0202M08
N260G70P70Q190
N270G28G40U0W0T0200M09
N280M30

Note: To use the single block format for program #O0014, omit line N50 and replace line N60 with: N100G72P70Q190U.015W.005D.06

CNC Turning Center Programming Exercise 15 Program Code

G73 Pattern Repeating Cycle

Programmed tool path using Pattern Repeating Cycle (G73).
 The dashed line on the drawing indicates the net shape of the part and the metal to be removed.
 Caution: DO NOT attempt to execute this program from solid bar stock.

A calculation is required to obtain the length of the tapered section.

.720 - .409 = .311
.311/2 = .1555
Length = .155 * TAN 75° = .5803

O0015
(CNC Turning Center Programming Exercise 15)
(Date, By)

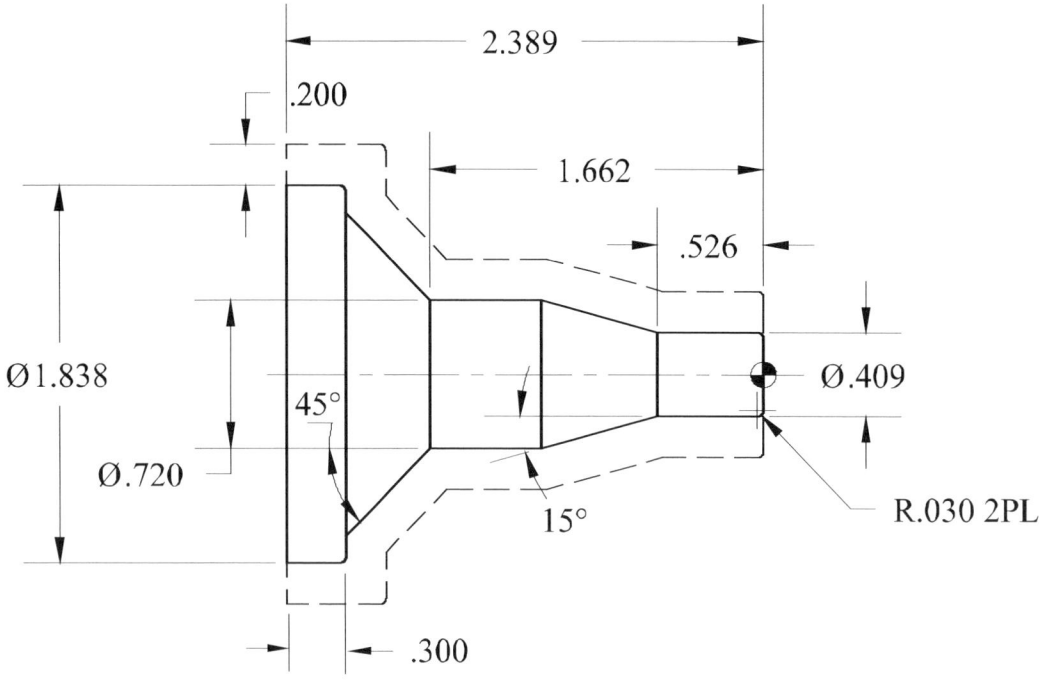

Figure 83 CNC Turning Center Programming Exercise 15

(Tool #1, Rough Turning Tool)
N10T0100
N20G96S513M3
N30G0G42X2.338Z.1T0101M08
N40G1Z.05F.0215
N50G73U.2W.2R3
N60G73P70Q160U.03W.005
N70G0X.349
N80G1Z0F.0215
N90G3X.409Z-.03R.03
N100G1Z-.526
N110X.72Z-1.1063
N120Z-1.662
N130X1.574Z-2.089
N140X1.778
N150G3X1.838Z-2.119R.03
N160G1X2.338
N170G28G40U0W0T0100
N180M01
(Tool #2, Finish Turning Tool)
N190T0200

N200G96S513M3
N210G0G42X2.338Z.1T0202M08
N220G1Z.05F.0215
N230G70P70Q160
N240G28G40U0W0T0200M09
N250M30

Note: To use the single block format for program #O0015, omit line N50 and replace line N60 with: N100G73P70Q160U.03W.005D3

CNC Turning Center Programming Exercise 16 Program Code

The same Pattern Repeating Cycle applied to internal boring using (G73).

<u>The dashed line on the drawing indicates the net shape of the part and the metal to be removed.</u> The .813 diameter has been predrilled in an earlier operation.

Caution: DO NOT attempt to execute this program from solid bar stock.

O0016
(CNC Turning Center
Programming Exercise 16)
(Date, By)
(Tool #3, Rough Boring Tool)
N10T0300
N20G96S513M3
N30G0G41X.713Z.1T0303M08
N40G1Z.05F.0215
N50G73U.2W.2R3
N60G73P70Q180U.03W.005
N70G0X2.869
N80G1Z0F.0215
N90G2X2.809Z-.03R.03
N100G1Z-.19
N110G3X2.689Z-.25R.06
N120G1X2.475
N130G2X2.532Z-.28R.03
N140G1Z-.625
N150X1.46Z-1.075
N160X1.063
N170G2X.813Z-1.2R.125
N180G1X.713
N190G28G40U0W0T0100

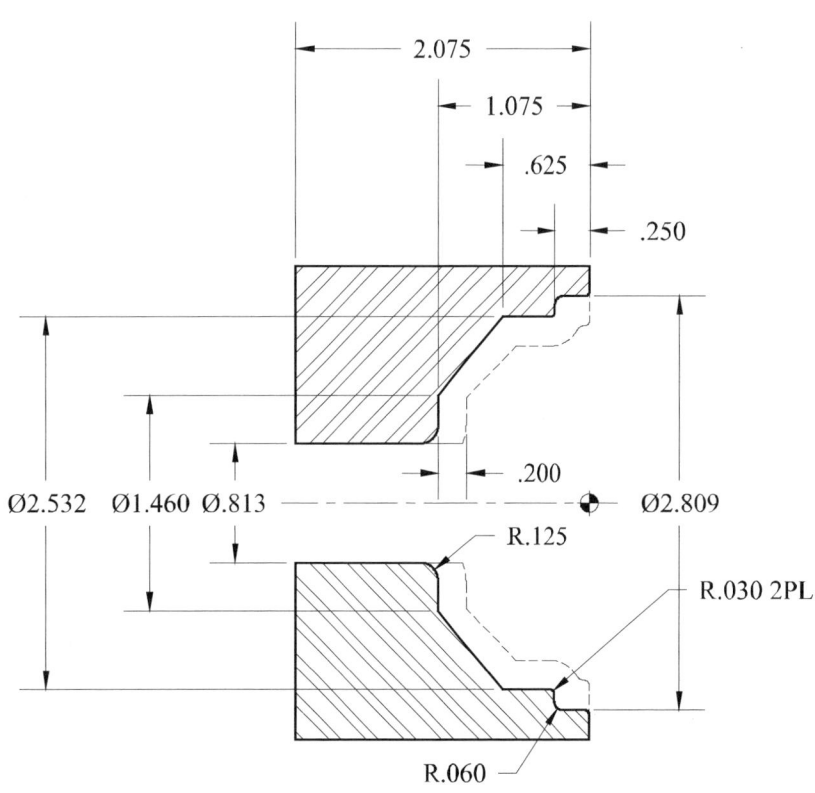

Figure 84
CNC Turning Center Programming Exercise 16

N200M01
(Tool #4, Finish Boring Tool)
N210T0400
N220G96S513M3
N230G0G42X2.338Z.1T0404M08
N240G1Z.05F.0215
N250G70P70Q180
N260G28G40U0W0T0200M09
N270M30
Note: To use the single block format for program #O0016, omit line N50 and replace line N60 with: N100G73P70Q180U.03W.005D3

Grooving

CNC Turning Center Programming Exercise 17 Program Code

G75

Programmed tool path using Groove Cutting Cycle (G75).

O0017
(CNC Turning Center Programming Exercise 17)
(Date, By)
(Tool #5, OD Grooving Tool .156 Wide)
N10T0500
N20G96S750M3
N30G0X1.53Z.1T0505M08
N40Z-.83
N50G75R.1
N60G75X1.23Z-1.03K.1
N70G0X1.53
N80G28G40U0W0T0500M09
N90M30

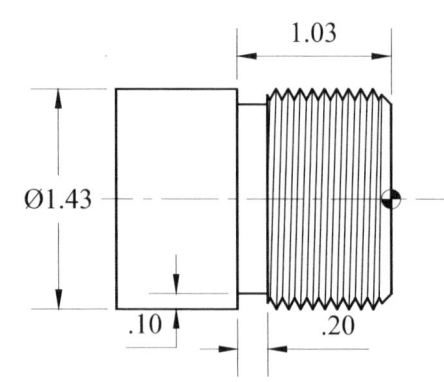

Figure 85
CNC Turning Center Programming Exercise 17

OD Threading

CNC Turning Center Programming Exercise 18 Program Code

G76 Threading Cycle

Programmed tool path using Threading Cycle (G76).

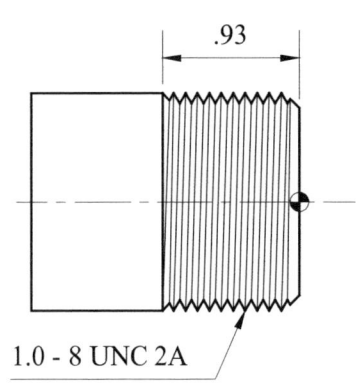

.93

1.0 - 8 UNC 2A

Figure 86
CNC Turning Center Programming
Exercise 18

O0018
(CNC Turning Center Programming Exercise 18)
(Date, By)
(Tool #7, OD Threading Tool)
N10T0700
N20G97S764M3
N30G0X1.1Z.1T0707M08
N40G76X.8492Z-.93K.0707D0150A60F.125
N50G28G40U0W0T0700M09
N60M30

CNC Turning Center Subprogram Application

CNC Turning Center Programming Exercise 19 Program Code

M98 and M99

Programmed tool path using linear and circular interpolation with the application of a subprogram call and return (M98 and M99).

O0019
(CNC Turning Center Programming Exercise 19)
(Date, By)
(Tool #5, OD Grooving Tool .156 Wide)
N10T0500
N20G50S6000
N30G96S2100M3
N40G0X1.9Z.1T0505M08
N50Z-.360

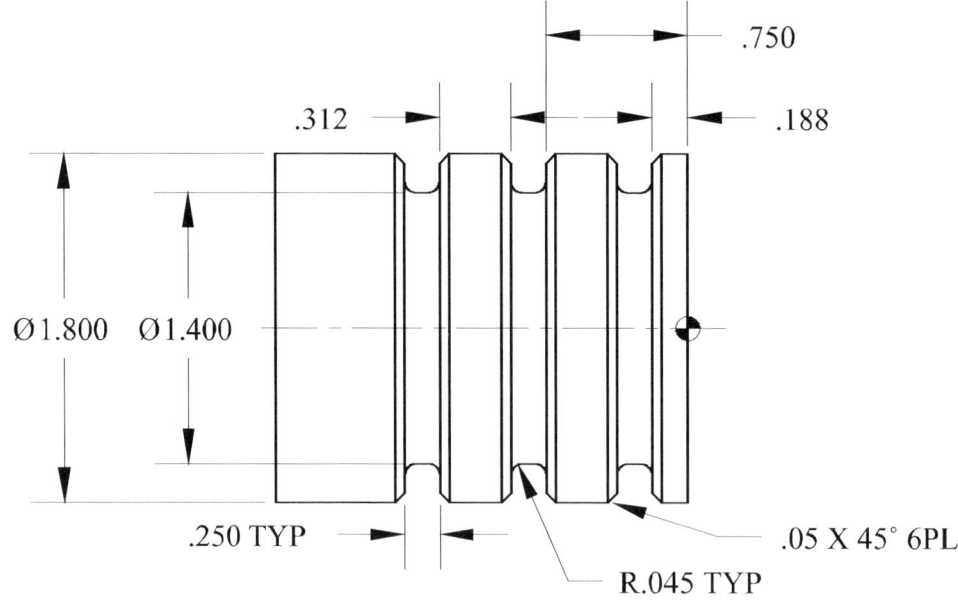

Figure 87 CNC Turning Center Programming Exercise 19

N60M98P3456L1
N70G0Z-.953
N80M98P3456L1
N90G0Z-1.906
N100M98P3456L1
N110G28G40U0W0T0500M09
N120M30

Subprogram for program O0019

O3456
N1G01X1.4F.0265
N2G0X1.9
N3Z-.291
N4G1X1.8F.013
N5U-.05W-.05
N6U-.105
N7G2U-.045W-.045R.045
N8G0X1.9

N9G1Z-.488
N10X1.8
N11U-.05W.05
N12U-.105
N13G3U-.045W.045R.045
N14G0X1.9
M99

CNC Turning Center Combined Project

CNC Turning Center Programming Exercise 20 Program Code

Programmed tool path using several Turning Cycles.

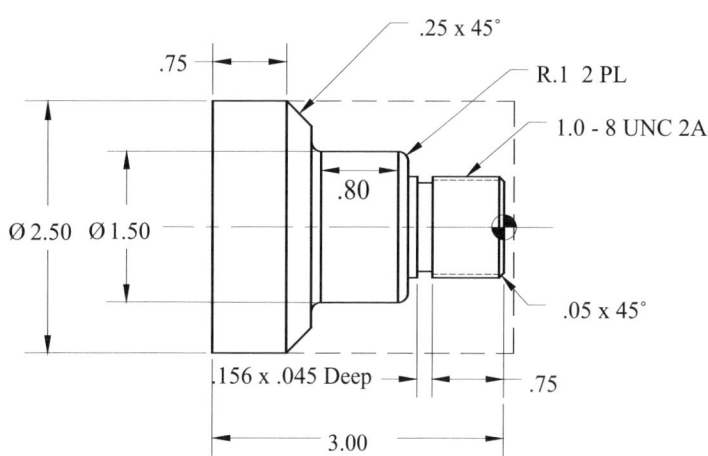

Figure 88
CNC Turning Center
Programming Exercise 20

Turning Center
CNC Setup Sheet

Date: Today	Prepared By: You
Part Name: Turning Center Project	Part Number: 1234
Machine: CNC Turning Center	Program Number:

Workpiece Zero: X = Centerline Y = NA Z = Finished Face

Setup Description:

Clamp the part in a 3-jaw chuck with soft-jaws, 2.35" minimum extended out of the chuck

Tool #	Tool Description	Offset #	Comments
1	Rough Turning Tool .031 TNRC	1	SFPM 125-1000
2	Finish Turning Tool .015 TNRC	2	SFPM 125-1000
5	O.D. Grooving Tool	5	.156 W ide .005 TNRC
7	O.D. Threading Tool	7	SFPM 125-1000

Facing Cut = r/min 191-1527
Turning 1.0 diameter, r/min = 477-3820
Turning 1.5 diameter, r/min = 318-2546
Turning 2.5 diameter, r/ min = 191-1528
Grooving .820 diameter, r/min = 582-4658
Threading r/min = 477-3820 Feed = Thread Lead

The preferred method of setting the r/min would be to use the Constant Cutting Speed (G96) command

O0020
(CNC Turning Center Programming Exercise 20)
(Date, By)
(Tool #1, Rough Turning Tool)
N10T0100
N20G50S6000
N30G96S563M3
N40G0X2.6Z.1T0101M08
N50G1Z0F.022
N60X-.02
N70G0Z.1
N80G42X.2.6
N90G71U.08R.1
N100G71P110Q210U.015W.005
N110G0X.90
N120G01Z0F.0265
N130X1.0Z-.05
N140Z-1.0
N150X1.3
N160G03X1.5Z-1.1R.1
N170G01Z-1.9
N180G2X1.7Z-2.0R.1
N190G01X2.0Z-2.0
N200X2.5Z-2.25
N210X2.6
N220G28G40U0W0T0100
N230M01
(Tool #2, Finish Turning Tool)
N240T0200
N250G50S6000
N260G96S563M3
N270G0G42X.90Z.1T0202M08
N280G1Z0F.022
N290G70P110Q210
N300G28G40U0W0T0200M09
N310M01
(Tool #5, OD Grooving Tool .156 Wide)
N320T0500
N330G96S563M3
N340G0X1.6Z-.906T0505M08

N350X1.1
N360G75R.1
N370G75X.82Z-.906I.09
N380G0X2.5
N390G28G40U0W0T0500M09
N400M01
(Tool #7, OD Threading Tool)
N410T0700
N420G97S1074M3
N430G0X1.1Z.1T0707M08
N440G76X.8492Z-.8K.0707D0150A60F.125
N450G28G40U0W0T0700M09
N460M30

Note: To use the single block format for program #O0020, omit line N90 and replace line N100 with:
N100G71P110Q210U.015W.005D.08

CNC Turning Center Program Error Diagnosis Answers

Use the skills you have learned to identify the problems in the following program lines and program sections. You may refer to the text, "Programming of CNC Machines" Third Edition.

1. Use the following CNC code and sketch a representation of the part being created.

O2001
(CNC Turning Center Program Diagnosis, Problem 1)
(Tool #1, Rough Turning Tool)
N10G50S2000
N15T0100M42
N20G96S500M03
N25G00X2.2Z.3T0101M08
N30G01Z.01F.03
N35X0.F.012
N40G00X3.0Z.2
N45G73P50Q85I.168K.169U.04W.02D3F.012
N50G00X1.59
N55G01Z0
N60X1.75Z-.08
N65Z-1.375
N70X2.0W-.125
N75Z-2.1
N80G03U.3Z-2.25I-.15K0.F.004
N85G01X2.75
N90Z-3.75
N95X2.85
N100G28U0W0T0100
N105M30

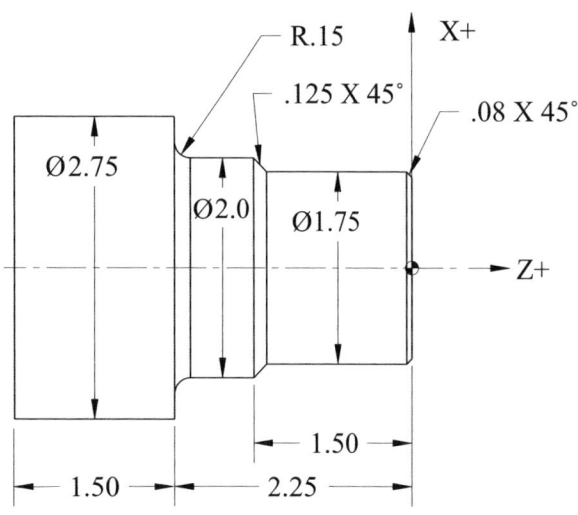

Figure 89
CNC Turning Center Programming Error
Diagnosis Part Drawing

2. Find the error in this program line.

   In line N100 the arc center coordinates or R for radius is missing.

N100G03U.3Z-2.25**I-.15K0.**F.004 or N100G03U.3Z-2.25**R.15**.F.004

3. Find the error in the following program lines.

   In line N40 the federate is missing for the G01 function.

O2003
(CNC Turning Center Program Diagnosis, Problem 3)
(Tool 9 = #5 Center Drill)
N10T0900
N20G97S641M03
N30G00X0Z.1T0909M08
N40G1Z-.4303**F.006**
N50G0Z.1M09
N60G28U0W0T0900
N70M30

4. Find the error in the following program section.

   In line N30 the spindle direction command is missing.

O2005
(CNC Turning Center Program Diagnosis, Problem 5)
(Tool #1, Rough Turning Tool)
N10T0100
N20G50S6000**M03**
N30G96S3650
N40G00X0Z.1T0101M08
. . . .
. . . .

5. Find the error in the following program.

 In line N60 the improper line numbers are called to execute the Multiple Repetitive Cycle.

O2005
(CNC Turning Center Program Diagnosis, Problem 5)
(Tool #3, Rough Boring Tool)
N10T0300

N20G50S6000
N30G96S2800M3
N40G0G41X.713Z.1T0303M08
N50G71U.08R.03
N60G71**P50Q150**U.015W.005
N70G0X2.192
N80G01Z0F.0265
N90G2X2.132Z-.03R.03
N100G01Z-.482
N110X1.714Z-.825
N120X1.209
N130X.813Z-1.025
N140X.713
N150G28G40U0W0T0300
N160M01

6. Find the error in the following program section.
     The program is missing a tool nose radius compensation call (T0101).

O2007
(CNC Turning Center Program Diagnosis, Problem 7)
(Tool #1, Rough Turning Tool)
N10T0100
N20G96S563M03
N30G00G41X.6975Z.1**T0101**M08
N40G1Z0F.022
N50X-.01
N60G0Z.1
N70G42X.4375

. . . .
. . . .

7. Find the error in the following program.
     In line N70 the tool nose radius compensation direction is incorrect. It should be G42.

O2008
(CNC Turning Center Program Diagnosis, Problem 7)
(Tool #1, Rough Turning Tool)
N10T0100
N20G96S563M03

N30G00G41X.6975Z.1T0101M08
N40G1Z0F.022
N50X-.01
N60G0Z.1
N70**G42**X.4375
N80G1Z0
N90X.875Z-.379
N100Z-.7
N110X1.438
N120X1.75Z-.856
N130Z-1.375
N140X2.09
N150X2.25Z-1.455
N160Z-2.25
N170G0X2.35Z.1M09
N180G28G40U0W0
N190M30

8. Find the error in the following program section.
       In line N100 re-initiation of G01 linear interpolation is missing.

O2009
(CNC Turning Center Program Diagnosis, Problem 8)
(Tool #1, Rough Turning Tool)
N10T0100
N20G50S6000
N30G96S2800M3
N40G0G42X2.005Z.1T0101M08
N50G72U.06R.1
N60G72P70Q190U.015W.015
N70G0Z0F.0265
N80X.28
N90G3X.4Z-.06R.06
N100**G01**Z-.125F.0265
N110X.8Z-.325
N120X1.185
N130G3X1.305Z-.385R.06
N140G01Z-.433
N150G2X1.365Z-.463R.03
N160G1X1.785
N170G3X1.905Z-.523R.06

N180G01Z-.563
N190X2.005
N200G28G40U0W0T0100
N210M01

9. Find the error in the following program section.
    In line N240 the cutting speed is missing from the Constant Surface Speed call.

(Tool #2, Finish Turning Tool)
N220T0200
N230G50S6000
N240G96M3
N250G0G42X.90Z.1T0202M08
N260G70P80Q190
N270G28G40U0W0T0200M09
N280M30

10. Find the error in the following program section.
    At the end of the finishing cycle the cutter compensation cancellation is missing.

(Tool #4, Finish Boring Tool)
N170T0400
N180G50S6000
N190G96S2800M3
N200G0G42X.90Z.1T0404M08
N210G70P80Q140
N220G28U0W0**T0400**M09
N230M30

CNC MACHINING CENTER PROGRAMMING ANSWERS

The answer programs given here are one method of machining the parts shown in the drawings. There are many possibilities for getting the correct results. The student should consult with their instructor for program verification and always proceed, with caution, when running a newly written program. In the following exercises where only one tool is required, a CNC Setup sheet is not necessary but the tool and setup information should be listed before your program code. Please use a CNC Setup sheet in all other cases for the sake of clarity.

CNC Machining Center Tool List

Face Mill, 3.0 inch diameter, 90°, 5 teeth, Carbide

End Mill, 2-Flute, 1/8 inch
End Mill, 2-Flute, 3/8 inch
End Mill, 2-Flute, 9/16 inch
End Mill, 2-Flute, 1 inch

End Mill, 4-Flute, 3/8 inch
End Mill, 4-Flute, 1/2 inch
End Mill, 4-Flute, 5/8 inch
End Mill, 4-Flute, 3/4 inch
End Mill, 4-Flute, 1 inch

Roughing End Mill, 4-Flute, 1 inch

#5 Center Drill
#6 Center Drill

Spotting Drill, .75 diameter, 90° single flute

Drill Bits, All sets are available in High Speed Steel

Taps, All sizes are available in High Speed Steel

Reamers, all required sizes are available in High Speed Steel

Programming Coordinate Identification for Milling Answers

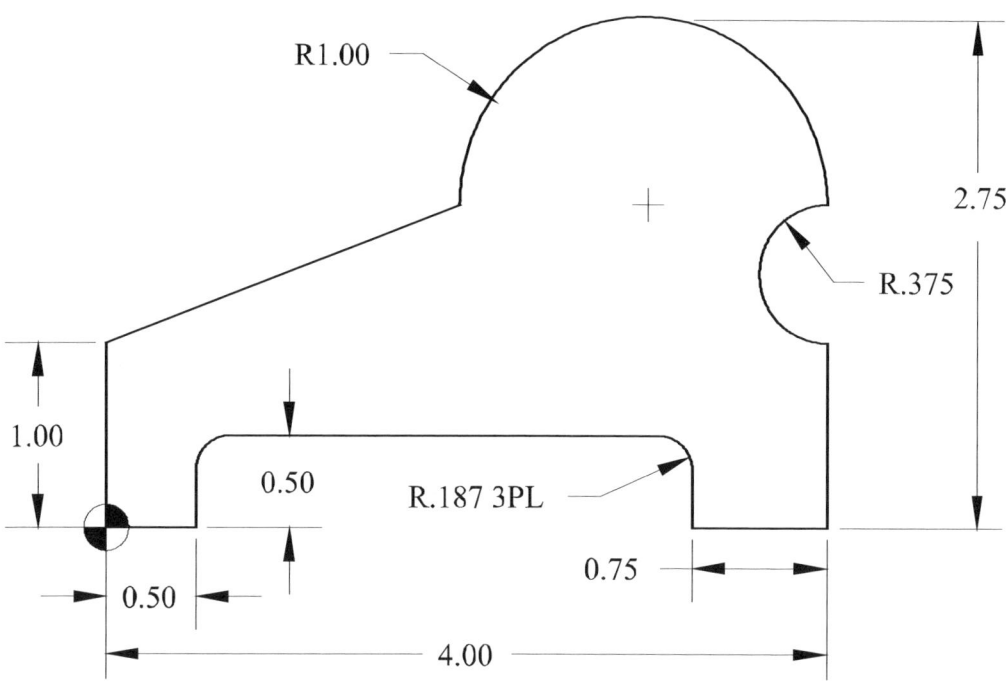

Figure 90 Answers for Absolute and Incremental Coordinates

1. Absolute programming coordinates, including the arc center locations.

X0Y0, X0Y1.0, X2.0Y1.75 (Arc Center X3.0Y1.75) X4.0Y1.75, (Arc Center X4.0Y1.375) X4.0Y1.0, X4.0Y0, X3.25Y0, X3.25Y.313 (Arc Center X3.063Y.313) X3.063Y.5, X.687Y.5, (Arc Center X.687Y.313) X.5Y.313, X.5Y0, X0Y0

2. Incremental programming coordinates, including the arc center locations.

X0Y0, X0Y1.0, X2.0Y.75 (Arc Center X1.0Y0) X2.0Y0, (Arc Center X0Y-.375) X0Y-75, X0Y-1.0, X-.75Y0, X0Y.5 (Arc Center X-.187Y.313) X-2.75Y0, (Arc Center X.687Y-.187) X0Y-.5, X-.5Y0

Linear Interpolation

Face Milling Exercises

CNC Machining Center Exercise #1 Program Code

Figure 91
CNC Machining Center Programming Exercise 1

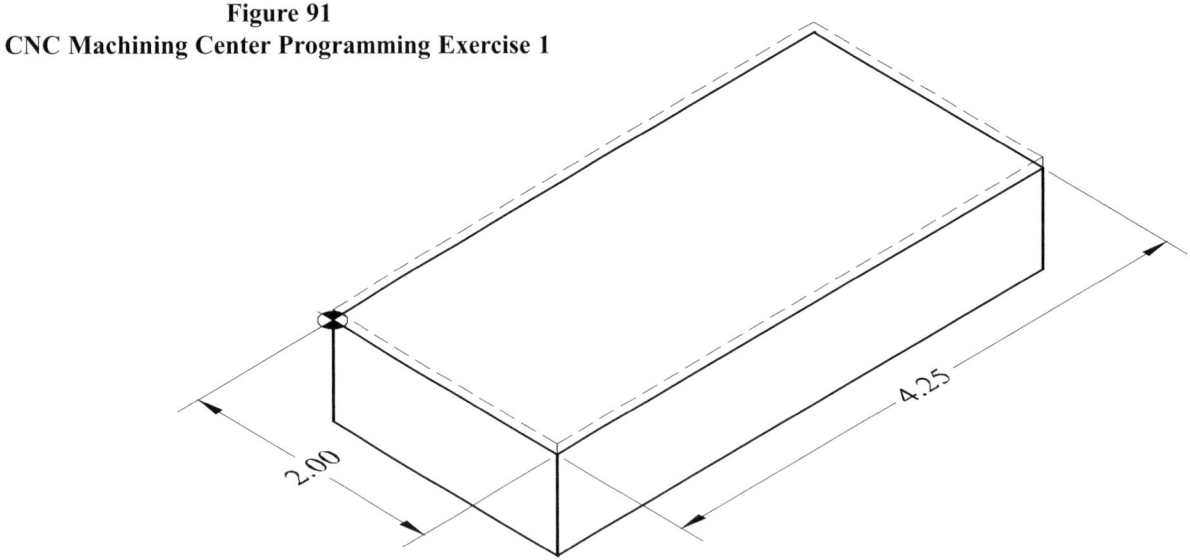

Programmed tool path using linear interpolation and rapid positioning (G01 and G00) for the Machining Center.

Tool = Face Mill, 3.0 inch diameter, 90°, 5 teeth, Carbide
Cutting Speed = 39-475
r/min = 50-605
in/tooth = .020-.039
in/min = 5.0-118

O0001
(CNC Machining Center Exercise #1)
(Date, by)
N10G90G20G80G40G49
(Tool #1 Face Mill, 3.0 inch diameter, 90°, 5 teeth, Carbide)
N20T01M06
N30S328M03
N40G54G0X5.85Y-.65
N50G43Z1.0H01
N60Z.1M08
N70Z-.08F10.0
N80X-1.6F49.0
N90G80Z.1M09
N100G91G28Z0
N110G28X0Y0
N120M30

Midrange feeds and speeds are used. On line N40, the Y-axis is positioned at -.5 in order that the tool is not positioned exactly on centerline. This is a better cutting method than positioning the tool on centerline. Consult the insert manufacturer catalogs to verify this technique.

CNC Machining Center Exercise #2 Program Code

Programmed tool path using linear interpolation and rapid positioning (G01 and G00) for the Machining Center.

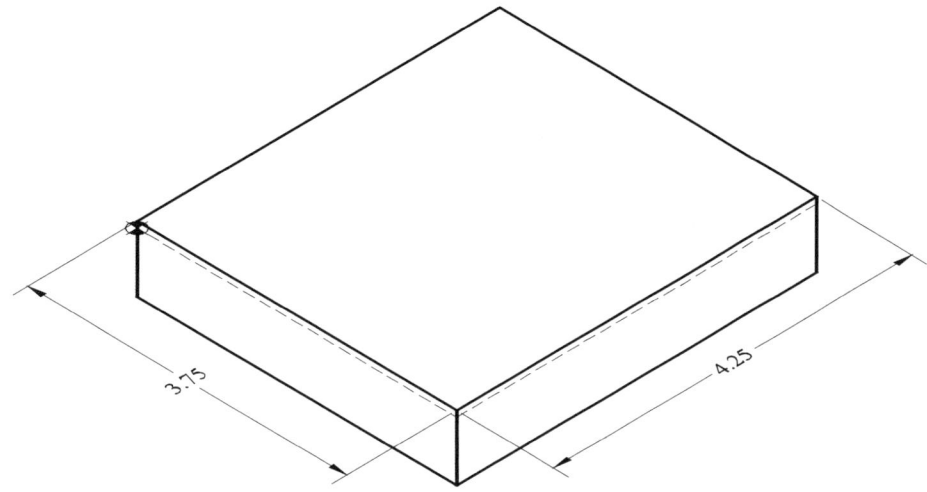

Figure 92 CNC Machining Center Programming Exercise 2

Tool = Face Mill, 3.0 inch diameter, 90°, 5 teeth, Carbide
Cutting Speed = 755-1720
r/min = 961-2190
in/tooth = .020-.039
in/min = 96.0-427.0

O0002
(CNC Machining Center Exercise #2)
(Date, by)
N10G90G20G80G40G49
(Tool #1 Face Mill, 3.0 inch diameter, 90°, 5 teeth, Carbide)
N20T01M06

N30S1575M03
N40G54G0X5.85Y-.5
N50G43Z1.0H01
N60Z.1M08
N70Z-.07F10.0
N80X-1.6F236.0
N90G0Z.1
N100X5.85Y-3.0
N110G01Z-.07F10.0
N120X-1.6F236.0
N90G80Z.1M09
N100G91G28Z0
N110G28X0Y0
N120M30

Midrange feeds and speeds are used.

Contour Milling

CNC Machining Center Exercise #3 Program Code

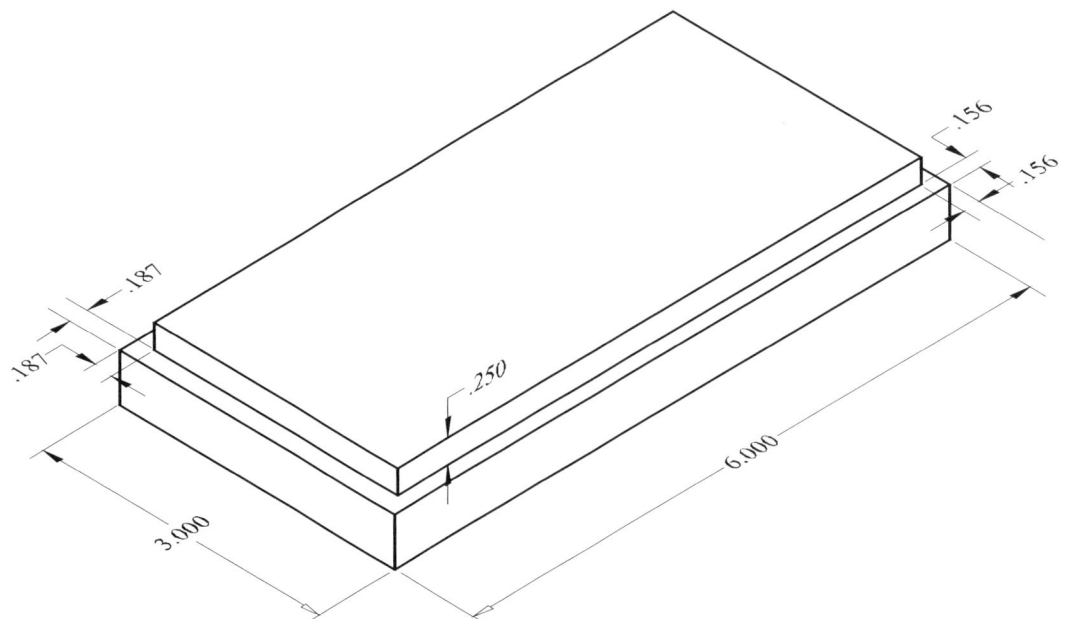

Figure 93 CNC Machining Center Programming Exercise 3

Programmed tool path for the part contour using linear interpolation and rapid positioning (G01 and G00) for the Machining Center.

Tool = .375 inch diameter, 4 flute, High Speed Steel, End Mill
Cutting Speed = 5-85
r/min = 51-865
in/tooth = .001-.004
in/min = .20-14.0

O0003
(CNC Machining Center Exercise #3)
(Date, By)
N10G90G20G80G40G49
(Tool #1 .375 inch diameter, 4 flute, High Speed Steel, End Mill)
N20T01M06
N30S458M03
N40G54G0X-.287Y0
N50G43Z1.0H01
N60Z.1M08
N70Z-.125F10.0
N80X6.031F7.0
N90Y-3.031
N100X0
N110Y.287
N120G0Z.1
N130X-.287Y0
N140Z-.25F10.0
N150X6.031F7.0
N160Y-3.031
N170X0
N180Y.287
N190G80Z.1M09
N200G91G28Z0
N210G28X0Y0
N220M30

Circular Interpolation

Contour Milling

CNC Machining Center Exercise #4 Program Code

Programmed tool path for the part contour using linear and circular interpolation and rapid positioning (G01, G02 and G00), for the Machining Center. Radius programming is given using the program words R, I and J.

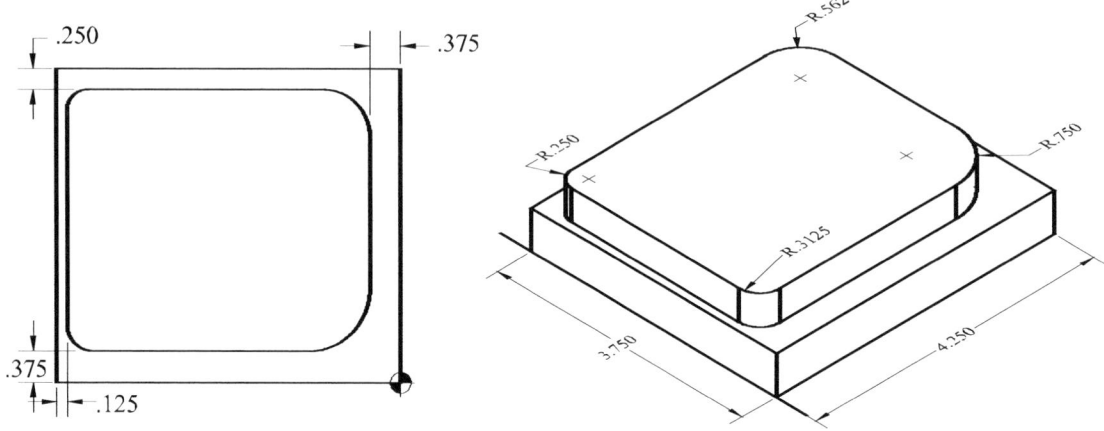

Figure 94 CNC Machining Center Programming Exercise 4

In the drawing below, it is shown that the 1.0 diameter end mill is necessary to accomplish the axial cut in one step.

**Figure 95
CNC Machining Center
Programming Exercise 4
Cutter Diameter Calculation**

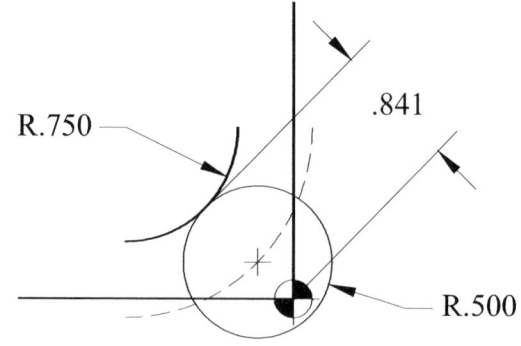

Tool = 1.00 inch diameter, 4 flute, High Speed Steel, End Mill
Cutting Speed = 5-85
r/min = 19-324
in/tooth = .001-.004
in/min = .076-5.2

The following program is written entirely using the R command for the radii.

O0004
(CNC Machining Center Exercise #4)
(Date, By)
N10G90G20G80G40G49
(Tool #1 1.0 inch diameter, 4 flute, High Speed Steel, End Mill)
N20T01M06
N30S172M03
N40G54G0X-4.625Y-.6
N50G43Z1.0H01
N60Z.1M08
N70G01Z-.1875F10.0
N80Y3.25F2.6
N90G2X-3.875Y4.R.75
N100G1X-.937
N110G2X.125Y2.938R1.062
N120G1Y1.125
N130G2X-1.125Y-.125R1.25
N140G1X-3.8125
N150G2X-4.625Y.6875R.8125
N160G1Z-.375
N170Y3.25
N180G2X-3.875Y4.R.75
N190G1X-.937
N200G2X.125Y2.938R1.062
N210G1Y1.125
N220G2X-1.125Y-.125R1.25
N230G1X-3.8125
N240G2X-4.625Y.6875R.8125
N250G80G0Z.1M09
N260G91G28Z0.
N270G28X0Y0
N280M30

The following program is written entirely using the I and J commands for the radii.

O0004
(CNC Machining Center Exercise #4)
(Date, By)
N10G90G20G80G40G49

(Tool #1 1.0 inch diameter, 4 flute, High Speed Steel, End Mill)
N20T01M06
N30S172M03
N40G54G0X-4.625Y-.6
N50G43Z1.0H01
N60Z.1M08
N70G01Z-.1875F10.0
N80Y3.25F2.6
N90G2X-3.875Y4.0I.75J0
N100G1X-.937
N110G2X.125Y2.938I0J-1.062
N120G1Y1.125
N130G2X-1.125Y-.125I-1.25J0
N140G1X-3.8125
N150G2X-4.625Y.6875I0J.813
N160G1Z-.375
N170Y3.25
N180G2X-3.875Y4.0 I.75J0
N190G1X-.937
N200G2X.125Y2.938I0J-1.062
N210G1Y1.125
N220G2X-1.125Y-.125I-1.25J0
N230G1X-3.8125
N240G2X-4.625Y.6875I0J.813
N250G80G0Z.1M09
N260G91G28Z0.
N270G28X0Y0
N280M30

CNC Machining Center Exercise #5 Program Code

Programmed tool path for the part contour using linear and circular interpolation and rapid positioning (G01, G02, G03 and G00), for the Machining Center. Radius programming is given using the program words R, I and J.

In this case, a .375 inch diameter end mill is used due to the three .1875 inch fillet radii required on the drawing.

Tool = .375 inch diameter, 2 flute, Carbide, End Mill
Cutting Speed = 600-2000

r/min = 6111-20372
in/tooth = .008-.015
in/min = 98.0-611.0

In this case, since the maximum r/min of the machine being used is 6000, this will be the r/min used in the program and the feed rates are adjusted accordingly.

The following drawing (Figure 97) indicates the necessary tool radius offset for the correct tool path in relation to the angled surface and the counterclockwise arc.

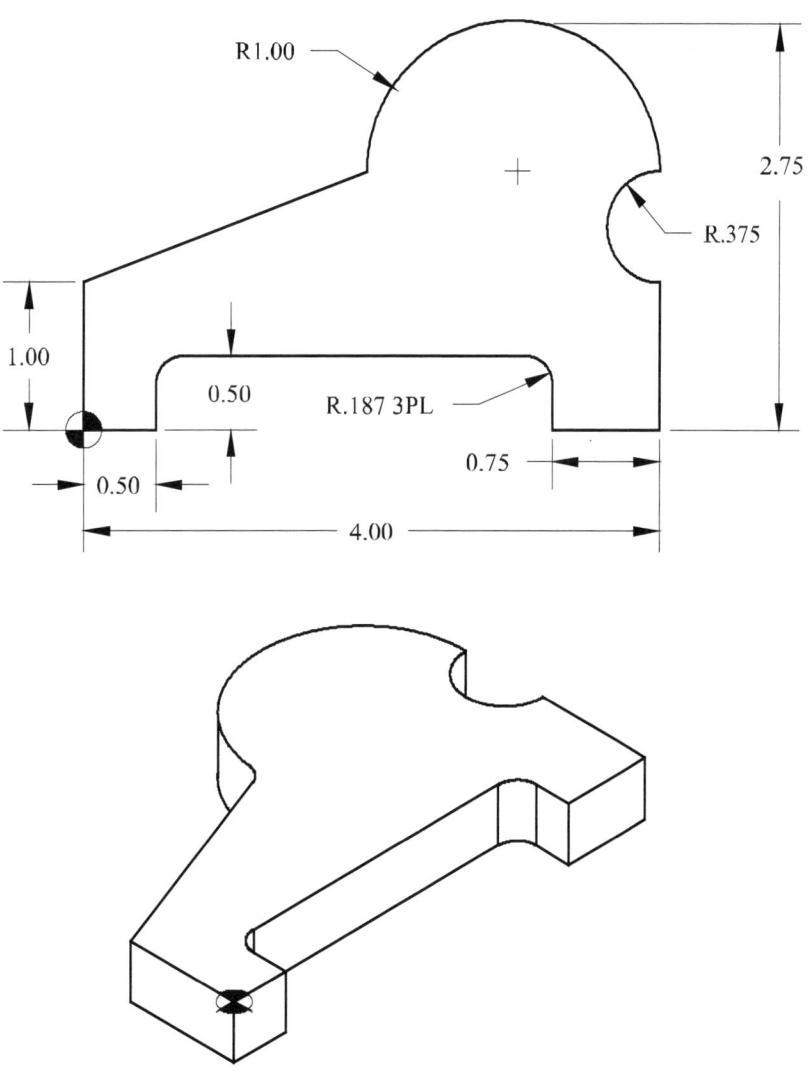

Figure 96
CNC Machining Center Programming Exercise 5

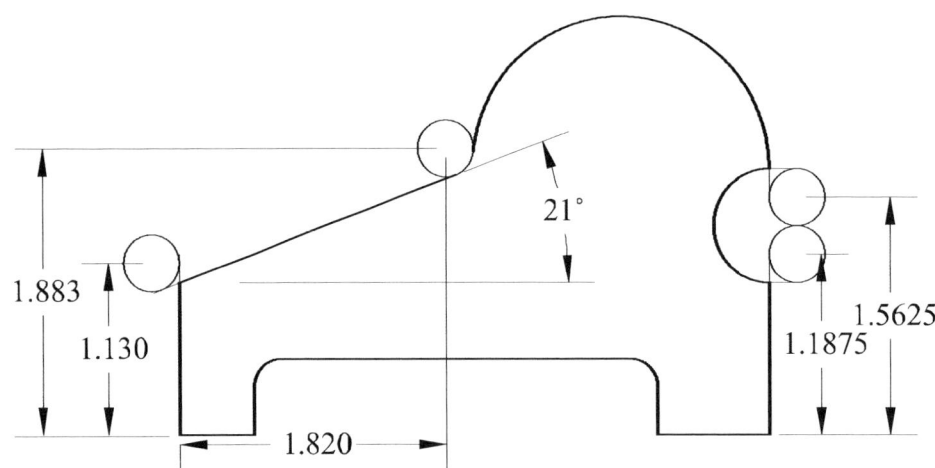

Figure 97 CNC Machining Center Programming Exercise 5 Cutter Location Coordinates

The following program is written entirely using the R command for the radii.

O0005
(CNC Machining Center Exercise #5)
(Date, By)
N10G90G20G80G40G49
(Tool #1 .375 inch diameter, 2 flute, Carbide, End Mill)
N20T01M06
N30S6000M03
N40G54G0X-.1875Y-.2875
N50G43Z1.0H01
N60Z.1M08
N70G1Z-.25F10.0
N80Y1.13F138.0
N90X1.82Y1.883
N100G2X4.1875Y1.75R1.1875
N110G1Y1.5625
N120X4.0
N130G3Y1.1875R.1875
N140G1X4.1875
N150Y-.1875
N160X3.0625
N170Y.3125
N180X.6875
N190Y-.1875

N200X-.2875
N210G0Z.1
N220X-.1875Y-.2875
N230G1Z-.5F10.0
N240Y1.13F138.0
N250X1.82Y1.883
N260G2X4.1875Y1.75R1.1875
N270G1Y1.5625
N280X4.0
N290G3Y1.1875R.1875
N300G1X4.1875
N310Y-.1875
N320X3.0625
N330Y.3125
N340X.6875
N350Y-.1875
N360X-.2875
N370G0Z.1
N380X-.1875Y-.2875
N390G80Z.1M09
N400G91G28Z0.
N410G28X0Y0
N420M30

The following program is written entirely using the I and J commands for the radii.

O0005
(CNC Machining Center Exercise #5)
(Date, By)
N10G90G20G80G40G49
(Tool #1 .375 inch diameter, 2 flute, Carbide, End Mill)
N20T01M06
N30S6000M03
N40G54G0X-.1875Y-.2875
N50G43Z1.0H01
N60Z.1M08
N70G1Z-.25F10.0
N80Y1.13F138.0
N90X1.82Y1.883
N100G2X4.1875Y1.75I1.1875J0
N110G1Y1.5625

N120X4.0
N130G3Y1.1875I0J-.1875
N140G1X4.1875
N150Y-.1875
N160X3.0625
N170Y.3125
N180X.6875
N190Y-.1875
N200X-.2875
N210G0Z.1
N220X-.1875Y-.2875
N230G1Z-.5F10.0
N240Y1.13F138.0
N250X1.82Y1.883
N260G2X4.1875Y1.75I1.1875J0
N270G1Y1.5625
N280X4.0
N290G3Y1.1875I0J-.1875
N300G1X4.1875
N310Y-.1875
N320X3.0625
N330Y.3125
N340X.6875
N350Y-.1875
N360X-.2875
N370G0Z.1
N380X-.1875Y-.2875
N390G80Z.1M09
N400G91G28Z0.
N410G28X0Y0
N420M30

Circle Milling

CNC Machining Center Exercise #6 Program Code

Programmed tool path for the part contour using linear and circular interpolation and rapid positioning (G01, G02, G03 and G00), for the Machining Center. Radius programming is given using the program words R, I and J.

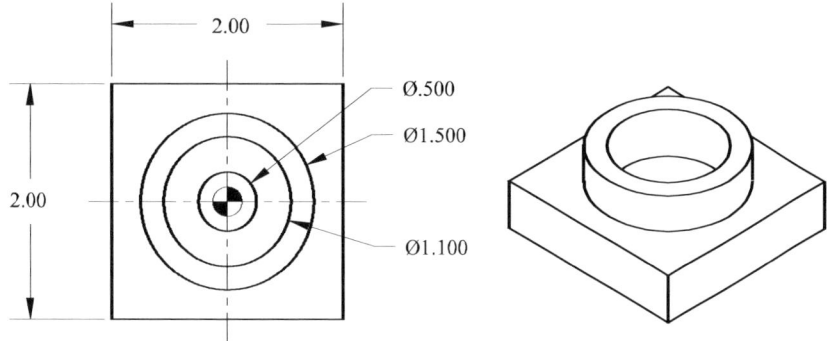

Figure 98 CNC Machining Center Programming Exercise 6

In the drawing below, it is shown that a .75 inch diameter end mill is necessary to accomplish the axial cut in one step.

Figure 99
CNC Machining Center Programming Exercise 6
Cutter Size Requirement Calculation

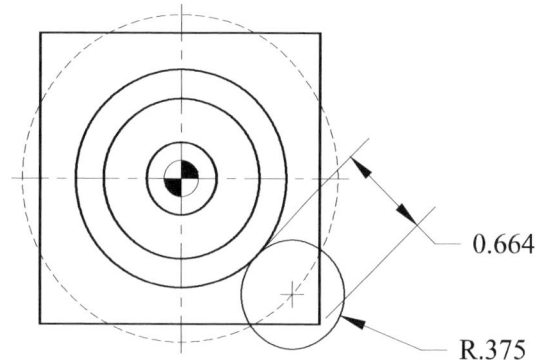

The following program is written entirely using the R command for the radii.

Tool = .75 inch diameter, 4 flute, HSS, End Mill
Cutting Speed = 25-140
r/min = 127-713
in/tooth = .001-.004
in/min = .508-11.4

O0006
(CNC Machining Center Exercise #6)
(Date, By)
N10G90G20G80G40G49
(Tool #1 .75 inch diameter, 4 flute, HSS, End Mill)
N20T01M06
N30S420M3
N40G54G0X1.375Y0
N50G43Z.1H1
N60Z.1M08

N70G01Z-.375F10.0
N80X1.125
N90G2X-1.125R1.125F5.96
N100X1.125R1.125
N110G0Z.1
N120X0Y0
N130G1Z-.5F10.0
N140X.175
N150G3X-.175R.175F5.96
N160X.175R.175
N170G80G0Z.1M09
N180G91G28Z0.
N190G28X0Y0
N200M30

The following program is the same program written entirely using the I and J commands for the radii.

O0006
(CNC Machining Center Exercise #6)
(Date, By)
N10G90G20G80G40G49
(Tool #1 .75 inch diameter, 4 flute, HSS, End Mill)
N20T01M06
N30S420M3
N40G54G0X1.375Y0
N50G43Z.1H1
N60Z.1M08
N70G01Z-.375F10.0
N80X1.125
N90G2X-1.125I-1.125J0F5.96
N100X1.125I1.125J0
N110G0Z.1
N120X0Y0
N130G1Z-.5F10.0
N140X.175
N150G3X-.175I-.175J0F5.96
N160X.175I.175J0
N170G80G0Z.1M09
N180G91G28Z0
N190G28X0Y0
N200M30

Cutter Diameter Compensation

Programmed tool path for the part contour of Machining Center exercises 3, 4, 5 and 6 with (G41, G42 and G40) cutter diameter compensation. Radius programming is given using the program words R, I and J.

CNC Machining Center Exercise #7 Program Code

Cutter Diameter Compensation for Exercise 3

Tool = .375 inch diameter, 4 flute, High Speed Steel, End Mill
Cutter Diameter Compensation offset # = D31
Cutting Speed = 5-85
r/min = 51-865
in/tooth = .001-.004
in/min = .20-14.0

O0007
(CNC Machining Center Exercise #7)
(Date, By)
N10G90G20G80G40G49
(Tool #1 .375 inch diameter, 4 flute, High Speed Steel, End Mill)
(Cutter Diameter Compensation offset #D31)
N20T01M06
N30S458M03
N40G54G0X-.2Y.2
N50G43Z1.0H01
N60Z.1M08
N70G1Z-.125F10.0
N80X0Y-.187G41D31
N90X5.813F7.0
N100Y-2.844
N110X.187
N120Y.187
N130G0Z.1
N140G0X-.2Y.2
N150G1Z-.25F10.0
N160X0Y-.187G41D31
N170X5.813F7.0
N180Y-2.844
N190X.187

N200Y.187
N210G0Z.1
N220G80G0Z.1M09
N230G40Y.375
N240G91G28Z0
N250G28X0Y0
N260M30

CNC Machining Center Exercise #8 Program Code

Cutter Diameter Compensation for Exercise 4

Tool = 1.00 inch diameter, 4 flute, High Speed Steel, End Mill
Cutter Diameter Compensation offset # = D31
Cutting Speed = 5-85
r/min = 19-324
in/tooth = .001-.004
in/min = .076-5.2

The following program is written entirely using the R command for the radii.

```
O0008
(CNC Machining Center Exercise #8)
(Date, By)
N10G90G20G80G40G49
(Tool #1 1.0 inch diameter, 4 flute, High Speed Steel, End Mill)
(Cutter Diameter Compensation offset #D31)
N20T01M06
N30S172M03
N40G54G0X-4.75Y-.6
N50G43Z1.0H01
N60Z.1M08
N70G01Z-.1875F10.0
N80X-4.125Y0G41D31
N90Y3.25F2.6
N100G2X-3.875Y3.5R.25
N110G1X-.937
N120G2X-.375Y2.938R.562
N130G1Y1.125
N140G2X-1.125Y.375R.75
N150G1X-3.8125
N160G2X-4.125Y.6875R.3125
N170G1Z-.375
N180Y3.25
N190G2X-3.875Y3.5R.25
N200G1X-.937
N210G2X-.375Y2.938R.562
N220G1Y1.125
N230G2X-1.125Y.375R.75
```

N240G1X-3.8125
N250G2X-4.125Y.6875R.3125
N260G80G0Z.1M09
N270G40X-4.75Y0
N280G91G28Z0
N290G28X0Y0
N300M30

The same program written entirely using the I and J commands for the radii.

O0008
(CNC Machining Center Exercise #8)
(Date, By)
N10G90G20G80G40G49
(Tool #1 1.0 inch diameter, 4 flute, High Speed Steel, End Mill)
(Cutter Diameter Compensation offset #D31)
N20T01M06
N30S172M03
N40G54G0X-4.75Y-.6
N50G43Z1.0H01
N60Z.1M08
N70G01Z-.1875F10.0
N75X-4.125Y0G41D31
N80Y3.25F2.6
N90G2X-3.875Y3.5I.25J0
N100G1X-.937
N110G2X-.375Y2.938I0J-.562
N120G1Y1.125
N130G2X-1.125Y.375I-.75J0
N140G1X-3.8125
N150G2X-4.125Y.688I0J.3125
N160G1Z-.375
N170Y3.25
N182G2X-3.875Y3.5I.25J0
N190G1X-.937
N200G2X-.375Y2.938I0J-.562
N210G1Y1.125
N220G2X-1.125Y.375I-.75J0
N230G1X-3.8125
N240G2X-4.125Y.688I0J.3125
N250G80G0Z.1M09

N260G40X-4.75Y0
N260G91G28Z0
N270G28X0Y0
N280M30

CNC Machining Center Exercise #9 Program Code

Cutter Diameter Compensation for Exercise 5

Tool = .375 inch diameter, 2 flute, Carbide, End Mill
Cutter Diameter Compensation offset # = D31
Cutting Speed = 600-2000
r/min = 6111-20372
in/tooth = .008-.015
in/min = 98.0-611.0

The following program is written entirely using the R command for the radii.

```
O0009
(CNC Machining Center Exercise #9)
(Date, By)
N10G90G20G80G40G49
(Tool #1 .375 inch diameter, 2 flute, Carbide, End Mill)
(Cutter Diameter Compensation offset #D31)
N20T01M06
N30S6000M03
N40G54G0X-.2Y-.2
N50G43Z1.0H01
N60Z.1M08
N70G1Z-.25F10.0
N80X0Y0G41D31
N90Y1.0F138.0
N100X2.0Y1.75
N110G2X4.0Y1.75R1.0
N120G3Y1.0R.375
N130G1Y0
N140X3.25
N150Y.50
N160X.50
N170Y0
N180X-.1875
N190G0Z.1
N200X-.3Y-.3
N210G1Z-.5F10.0
N220X0Y0G41D31
N230Y1.0F138.0
```

N240X2.0Y1.75
N250G2X4.0Y1.75R1.0
N260G3Y1.0R.375
N270G1Y0
N280X3.25
N290Y.5
N300X.5
N310Y0
N320X0
N330G0Z.1
N340G40X-.4-.4
N350G80Z.1M09
N360G91G28Z0
N370G28X0Y0
N380M30

The same program is written entirely using the I and J commands for the radii.

O0009
(CNC Machining Center Exercise #5)
(Date, By)
N10G90G20G80G40G49
(Tool #1 .375 inch diameter, 2 flute, Carbide, End Mill)
(Cutter Diameter Compensation offset #D31)
N20T01M06
N30S6000M03
N40G54G0X-.2Y-.2
N50G43Z1.0H01
N60Z.1M08
N70G1Z-.25F10.0
N80X0Y0G41D31
N90Y1.0F138.0
N100X2.0Y1.75
N110G2X4.0Y1.75I1.0J0
N120G3Y1.0I0J-.375
N130G1Y0
N140X3.25
N150Y.50
N160X.50
N170Y0
N180X0

N190G0Z.1
N200X-.4Y-.4
N220Z-.5F10.0
N210G1X0Y0
N230Y1.0F138.0
N240X2.0Y1.75
N250G2X4.0Y1.75I1.0J0
N260G3Y1.0I0J-.375
N270G1Y0
N280X3.25
N290Y.5
N300X.5
N310Y0
N320X0
N330G0Z.1
N340G40X-.4-.4
N330G80Z.1M09
N350G91G28Z0.
N360G28X0Y0
N370M30

CNC Machining Center Exercise #10 Program Code

Cutter Diameter Compensation for Exercise 6

Tool = .75 inch diameter, 4 flute, HSS, End Mill
Cutting Speed = 25-140
r/min = 127-713
in/tooth = .001-.004
in/min = .508-11.4

The following program is written entirely using the R command for the radii.

O0010
(CNC Machining Center Exercise #10)
(Date, By)
N10G90G20G80G40G49
(Tool #1 .75 inch diameter, 4 flute, HSS, End Mill)
(Cutter Diameter Compensation offset #D31)
N20T01M06
N30S420M3

```
N40G54G0X1.5Y0
N50G43Z.1H1
N60Z.1M08
N70G01Z-.375F10.0
N80X.75G41D31F5.96
N90G2X-.75R.75
N100X.75R.75
N110G0G40Z.1
N120X0Y0
N130G1Z-.5F10.0
N140X.55Y0G41D31
N150G3X-.55R.55
N160X.55R.55
N170G80G0Z.1M09
N180G40X-.1
N190G91G28Z0.
N200G28X0Y0
N210M30
```

The same program is written entirely using the I and J commands for the radii.

```
O0010                                          N160X.55I.55J0
(CNC Machining Center Exercise #10)            N170G80G0Z.1M09
(Date, By)                                     N180G40X-.1
N10G90G20G80G40G49                             N190G91G28Z0.
(Tool #1 .75 inch diameter, 4 flute, HSS, End Mill)   N200G28X0Y0
(Cutter Diameter Compensation offset #D31)
N20T01M06
N30S420M3
N40G54G0X1.5Y0
N50G43Z.1H1
N60Z.1M08
N70G01Z-.375F10.0
N80X.75G41D31F5.96
N90G2X-.75I-.75J0
N100X.75I.75J0
N110G40G0Z.1
N120X0Y0
N130G1Z-.5F10.0
N140X.55G41D31F5.96
N150G3X-.55I-.55J0
```

Canned Cycles

CNC Machining Center Exercise #11 Program Code
G81 Drilling

Programmed tool path for the drilled hole using Canned Cycle (G81 and G00), for the Machining Center. This program segment could be added to the beginning of the program for CNC Machining Center Exercise #6 to aid the entry of the end mill.

Calculation is necessary to allow for the drill point.

.25 * TAN 31° = .150

.500 – .150 = .350 for the drill depth

Tool = .5 inch diameter, HSS, Drill
Cutting Speed = 25-140
r/min = 190-1070
in/tooth = .001-.004
in/min = .38-8.5

O0011
(CNC Machining Center Exercise #11)
(Date, By)
N10G90G20G80G40G49
(Tool #1 .#5 Center Drill)
N20T01M06
N30S630M03
N40G54G0X0Y0
N50G43Z1.0H01
N60Z.1M08
N70G81G99Z-.25R.1F4.0
N80G80Z.1M09
N90G91G28Z0
N100G28X0Y0
(Tool #2 .5 inch diameter, HSS, Drill)
N110T01M06
N12030S630M03
N130G54G0X0Y0
N140G43Z1.0H02
N150Z.1M08

N160G81G99Z-.35R.1F4.0
N170G80Z.1M09
N180G91G28Z0
N190G28X0Y0
(Tool #3 .75 inch diameter, 4 flute, HSS, End Mill)
N200T03M06
N210S420M3
N220G54G0X1.375Y0
N230G43Z.1H3
N240Z.1M08
N250G01Z-.375F10.0
N260X1.125
N270G2X-1.125R1.125F5.96
N280X1.125R1.125
N290G0Z.1
N300X0Y0
N310G1Z-.5F10.0
N320X.175
N330G3X-.175R.175F5.96
N340X.175R.175
N350G80G0Z.1M09
N360G91G28Z0.
N370G28X0Y0
N380M30

CNC Machining Center Exercise #12 Program Code
G81 & G73 Drilling

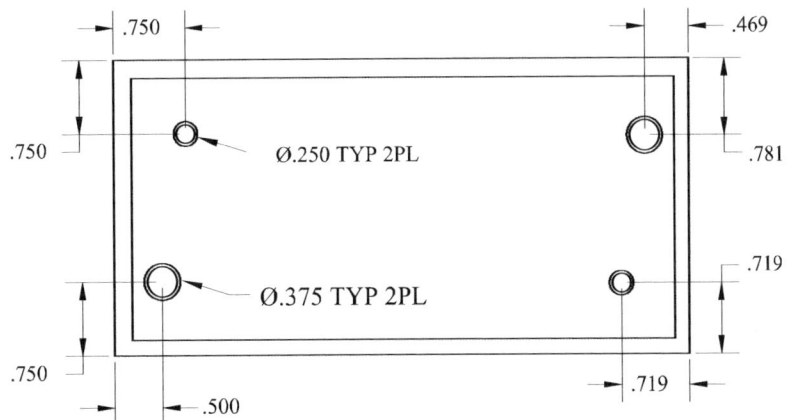

Figure 100 CNC Machining Center Programming Exercise 12

The holes are added to the existing program for CNC Machining Center Exercise 7, using Canned Drilling Cycles (G81, G73 and G80).

Tool 1 = .375 diameter, 4 flute, HSS End Mill
Cutter Diameter Compensation offset #D31
Cutting Speed = 5-85
r/min = 51-865
in/tooth = .001-.004
in/min = .20-14.0

Tool 2 = .75 diameter 90° HSS Spot Drill
Cutting Speed = 5-85
r/min = 25-433
in/tooth = .001-.004
in/min = .0025-1.73

Tool 3 = .25 diameter HSS Drill
Cutting Speed = 5-85
r/min = 76-1299
in/tooth = .001-.004
in/min = .152-10.4

Tool 4 = .375 diameter HSS Drill
Cutting Speed = 5-85
r/min = 51-865
in/tooth = .001-.004
in/min = .20-14.0

Calculation required for the Spot Drill depth on the .25 diameter hole.
.280/2 = .140 * TAN 45° = .140

Calculation required for the Spot Drill depth on the .375 diameter hole.
.405/2 = .2025 * TAN 45° = .2025

Calculation required to add for the drill point on the .25 diameter hole.
.250/2 = .125 * TAN 31° = .075

Calculation required, to add for the drill point on the .375 diameter hole.
.375/2 = .1875 * TAN 31° = .113

O0012
(CNC Machining Center Exercise #12)
(Date, By)
N10G90G20G80G40G49
(Tool #1 .375 inch diameter, 4 flute,
   High Speed Steel, End Mill)
(Cutter Diameter Compensation offset #D31)
N20T01M06
N30S458M03
N40G54G0X-.2Y.2
N50G43Z1.0H01
N60Z.1M08
N70G1Z-.125F10.0
N80X0Y-.187G41D31
N90X5.813F7.0
N100Y-2.844
N110X.187
N120Y.187
N130G0Z.1
N140X-.2Y.2
N150G1Z-.25F10.0
N160X0Y-.187G41D31
N170X5.813F7.0
N180Y-2.844
N190X.187
N200Y.187
N210G0Z.1
N220G80G0Z.1M09
N230G40Y.375
N240G91G28Z0
N250G28X0Y0
N260M01
(Tool 2 = .75 diameter 90° HSS Spot Drill)
N270T02M06
N280S230M03
N290G90G20G80G40G49
N300G54G0X.75Y-.75
N310G43Z1.0H02
N320Z.1M08
N330G81G99Z-.14R.1F1.0
N340X5.281Y-2.281

N350G81G99X5.531Y-.781Z-.2025R.1
N360X.5Y-3.25
N370G80Z.1M09
N380G91G28Z0
N390M01
(Tool 3 = .25 diameter HSS Drill)
N400T03M06
N410S688M03
N420G90G20G80G40G49
N430G54G0X.75Y-.75
N440G43Z1.0H03
N450Z.1M08
N460G73G99Z-.825Q.17R.1F3.44
N470X5.281Y-2.281
N480G80Z.1M09
N490G91G28Z0
N500M01
(Tool 4 = .375 diameter HSS Drill)
N510T04M06
N520S458M03
N530G90G20G80G40G49
N540G54G0X5.531Y-.781
N550G43Z1.0H03
N560Z.1M08
N570G73G99Z-.863Q.25R.1F7.0
N580X.5Y-2.25
N590G80Z.1M09
N600G91G28Z0
N610G28X0Y0
N620M30

CNC Machining Center Exercise #13 Program Code

G81, G83 and G82 Drilling

The holes are added to the existing program for CNC Machining Center Exercise 8, using Canned Drilling Cycles (G81, G83, G82 and G80).

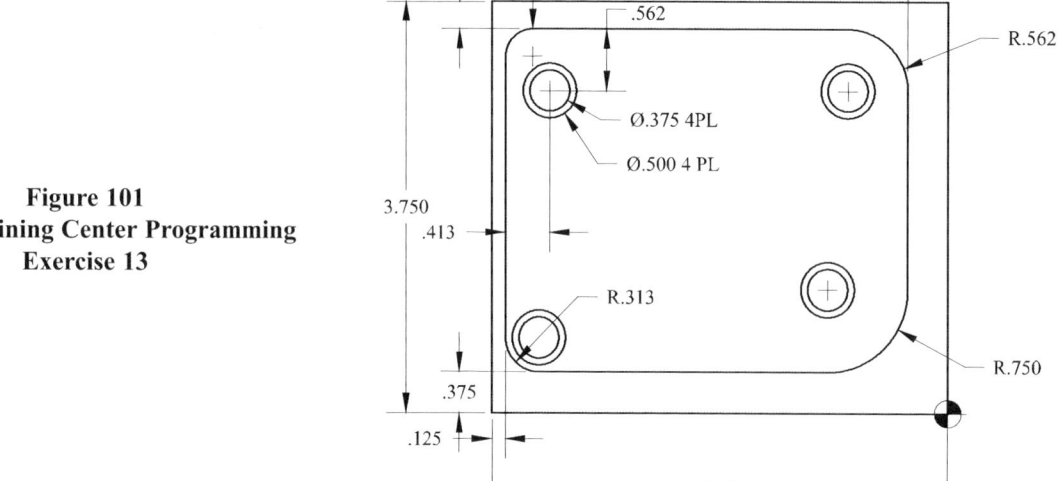

Figure 101
CNC Machining Center Programming
Exercise 13

Tool 1 = 1.00 inch diameter, 4 flute, High Speed Steel, End Mill
Cutter Diameter Compensation offset # = D31
Cutting Speed = 5-85
r/min = 19-324
in/tooth = .001-.004
in/min = .076-5.2

Tool 2 = #6 Center Drill
Cutting Speed = 5-85
r/min = 38-650
in/tooth = .001-.004
in/min = .076-5.2

Tool 3 =.375 inch diameter, HSS, Drill
Cutting Speed = 5-85
r/min = 51-866
in/tooth = .001-.004
in/min = .102-7.0

A calculation is necessary to allow addition for the drill point.

.1875 * TAN 31° = .113

1.0 + .113 = 1.13 for the drill depth

Tool 4 =.50 inch diameter, 4 flute, HSS, End Mill
Cutting Speed = 5-85
r/min = 19-324
in/tooth = .001-.004
in/min = .076-5.2

O0013
(CNC Machining Center Exercise #13)
(Date, By)
N10G90G20G80G40G49
(Tool #1 1.0 inch diameter, 4 flute, High Speed Steel, End Mill)
(Cutter Diameter Compensation offset #D31)
N20T01M06
N30S172M03
N40G54G0X-4.75Y-.6
N50G43Z1.0H01
N60Z.1M08
N70G01Z-.1875F10.0
N80X-4.125Y0G41D31
N90Y3.25F2.6
N100G2X-3.875Y3.5R.25
N110G1X-.937
N120G2X-.375Y2.938R.562
N130G1Y1.125
N140G2X-1.125Y.375R.75
N150G1X-3.8125
N160G2X-4.125Y.6875R.3125
N170G1Z-.375
N180Y3.25
N190G2X-3.875Y3.5R.25
N200G1X-.937
N210G2X-.375Y2.938R.562
N220G1Y1.125
N230G2X-1.125Y.375R.75
N240G1X-3.8125

N250G2X-4.125Y.6875R.3125
N260G80G0Z.1M09
N270G40X-4.75Y0
N280G91G28Z0
N290G28X0Y0
N290M01
(Tool 2 #6 Center Drill)
N300T01M06
N310S344M03
N320G90G20G80G40G49
N330G54G0X-1.125Y1.125
N340G43Z1.0H02
N350Z.1M08
N360G81G99Z-.4R.1F1.72
N370X-.937Y2.938
N380X-3.875
N390X-3.812Y.688
N400G80Z.1M09
N410G91G28Z0
N420M01
(Tool 3 .375 inch diameter, HSS, Drill)
N430T03M06
N440S459M03
N450G90G20G80G40G49
N460G54G0X-1.125Y1.125
N470G43Z1.0H03
N480Z.1M08
N490G83G99Z-1.13Q.25R.1F2.3
N500X-.937Y2.938
N510X-3.875
N520X-3.812Y.688
N530G80Z.1M09
N540G91G28Z0
N550M01
(Tool 4 .50 inch diameter, 4 flute, HSS End Mill)
N560T04M06
N570S172M03
N580G90G20G80G40G49
N590G54G0X-1.125Y1.125
N600G43Z1.0H03
N610Z.1M08

N620G82G99Z-.375P200R.1F2.6
N630X-.937Y2.938
N640X-3.875
N650X-3.812Y.688
N660G80Z.1M09
N670G91G28Z0
N680G28X0Y0
N690M30

CNC Machining Center Exercise #14 Program Code

G81, G82, G83 and G84

The holes programmed using Canned Drilling Cycles (G81, G82, G83, G84 and G80).

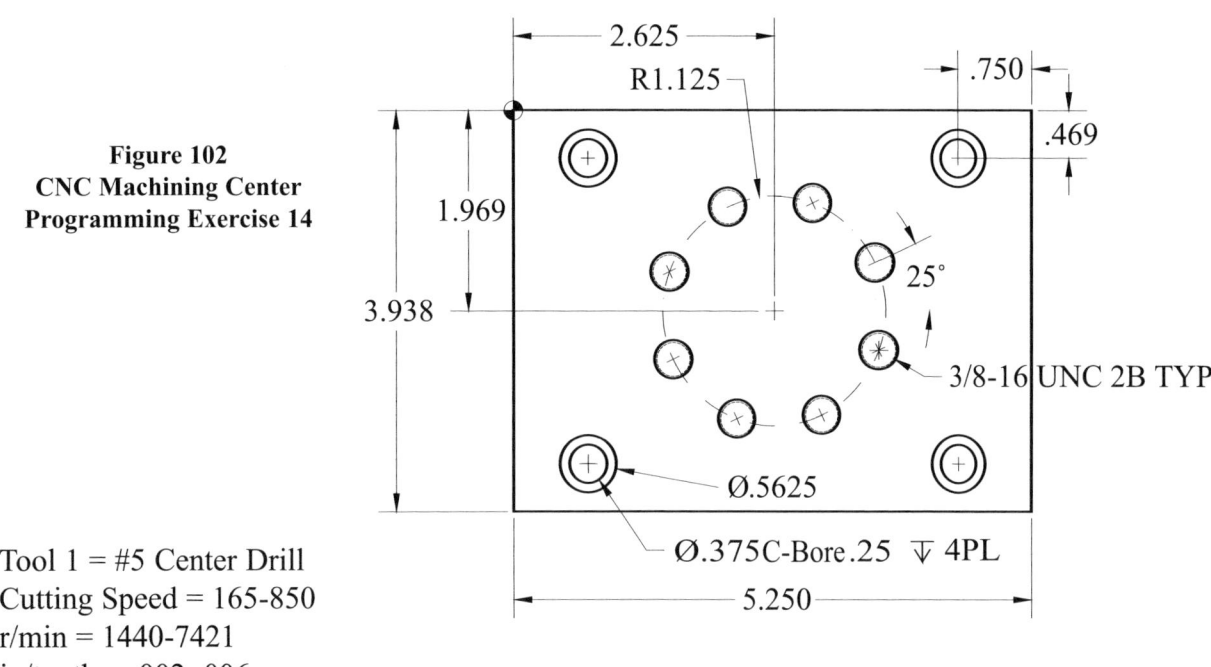

Figure 102
CNC Machining Center
Programming Exercise 14

Tool 1 = #5 Center Drill
Cutting Speed = 165-850
r/min = 1440-7421
in/tooth = .002-.006
in/min = 5.8-89.0

Calculations are necessary to allow addition for the Center Drill point to allow for a .395 inch diameter countersink for the thread lead.

.0938 * TAN 30° = .054 (for the 120° tip)
.1038 * TAN 60° = .1798 (for the 60° portion)
.054 + .1798 + .1875 = .4213

Tool 2 = 5/16 inch diameter, HSS, Drill
Cutting Speed = 165-850
r/min = 2017-10390
in/tooth = .002-.006
in/min = .8.0-125.0

A calculation is necessary to allow addition for the drill point.

.1563 * TAN 31° = .0939

+ .0939 = 1.0939 for the drill depth

Tool 3 = 3/8-16 TAP
Cutting Speed = 85
r/min = 865

A calculation for the feed is necessary and considers the use of a floating-type tap holder.

865 * 1/16 = 54.0

PROCEED WITH CAUTION

Tool 4 =.375 inch diameter, HSS, Drill
Cutting Speed = 165-850
r/min = 1681-8658
in/tooth = .002-.006
in/min = 6.7-104.0

A calculation is necessary to allow addition for the drill point.

.1875 * TAN 31° = .113

1.0 + .113 = 1.13 for the drill depth

Tool 5 =.5625 inch diameter, HSS, End Mill
Cutting Speed = 165-850
r/min = 1120-5772
in/tooth = .002-.006
in/min = 4.5-69.0

In the drawing below the coordinates for the Bolt Hole Circle are given.

O0014
(CNC Machining Center Exercise #14)
(Date, By)
N10G90G20G80G40G49
(Tool 1 #5 Center Drill)
N20T01M06

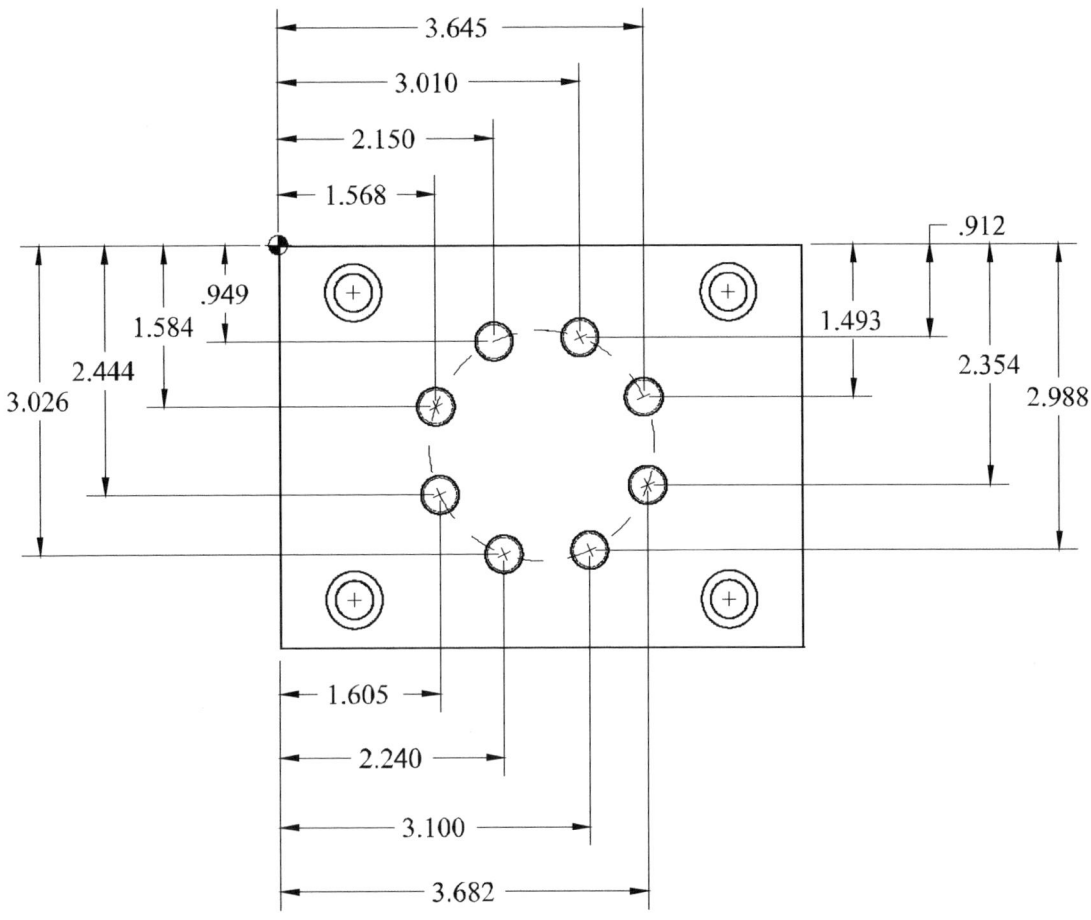

Figure 103 CNC Machining Center Programming Exercise 14 Coordinates

N30S4431M03
N40G90G20G80G40G49
N50G54G0X.75Y-.469
N60G43Z1.0H01
N70Z.1M08
N80G81G99Z-.4213R.1F47.0
N90Y-3.469
N100X4.5
N110Y-.469
N120X3.010Y-.912
N130X3.645Y-1.493

N140X3.682Y-2.354
N150X3.10Y-2.988
N160X2.24Y-3.026
N170X1.605Y-2.444N180X1.568Y-1.584
N190X2.15Y-.949
N200G80Z.1M09
N210G91G28Z0
N220M01
(Tool 2 5/16 inch diameter, HSS, Drill)
N230T02M06
N240S6000M03

N60G43Z1.0H02
N70Z.1M08
N80G83G99Z-1.094R.1F47.0
N90X3.645Y-1.493
N100X3.682Y-2.354
N110X3.10Y-2.988
N120X2.24Y-3.026
N130X1.605Y-2.444
N140X1.568Y-1.584
N150X2.15Y-.949
N160G80Z.1M09
N170G91G28Z0
N180M01
(Tool 3 3/8-16 TAP)
N190T03M06
N200S865M03
N210G90G20G80G40G49
N220G54G0X3.010Y-.912
N230G43Z1.0H03
N240Z.1M08
N250G84G99Z-1.2R.1F54.0
N260X3.645Y-1.493
N270X3.682Y-2.354
N280X3.10Y-2.988
N290X2.24Y-3.026
N300X1.605Y-2.444
N310X1.568Y-1.584
N320X2.15Y-.949
N330G80Z.1M09
N340G91G28Z0
N350M01

(Tool 4 3/8 diameter drill)
N360T04M06
N370S5169M03
N380G90G20G80G40G49
N390G54G0X.75Y-.469
N400G43Z1.0H04
N410Z.1M08
N420G83G99Z-1.13Q.25R.1F41.0
N430Y-3.469
N440X4.5
N450Y-.469
N460G80Z.1M09
N470G91G28Z0
N480M01
(Tool 5 9/16 2 flute End Mill)
N490T05M06
N500S3446M03
N510G90G20G80G40G49
N520G54G0X.75Y-.469
N530G43Z1.0H05
N540Z.1M08
N550G82G99Z-.25P200R.1F28.0
N560Y-3.469
N570X4.5
N580Y-.469
N590G80Z.1M09
N600G91G28Z0
N610G80Z.1M09
N620G91G28Z0
N630G28X0Y0
N640M30

CNC Machining Center Combined Projects

CNC Machining Center Exercise #15 Program Code

Program code for the Machining Center part in the Process Planning section of this workbook. The face mill tool path is programmed without the use of cutter radius compensation.

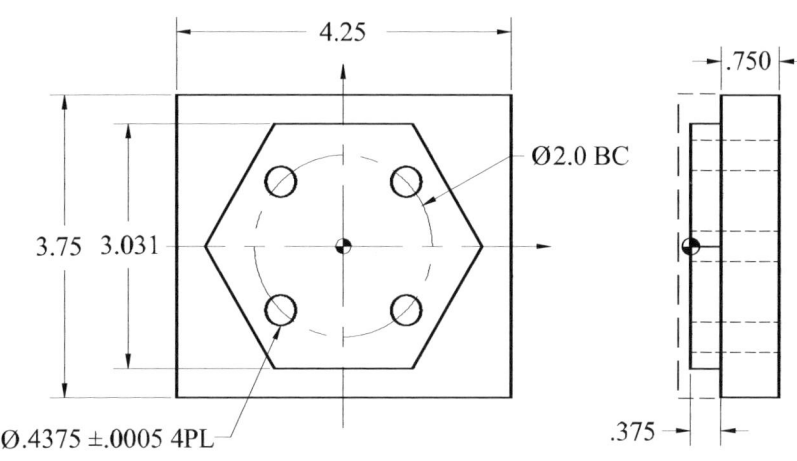

Figure 104
CNC Machining Center
Programming Exercise 15

Since the finished surface must be zero, it is required to touch off the raw material and then set the Z-offset value at -.100 inch.

Tool 1 = Face Mill, 3.0 inch diameter, 90°, 5 teeth, Carbide)
Cutting Speed = 755-1720
r/min = 961-2190
in/tooth = .020-.039
in/min = 96.0-335.0

Tool 2 = 1.0 inch diameter, HSS, 2 Flute End Mill
Cutting Speed = 165-850
r/min = 630-3247
in/tooth = .002-.006
in/min = 2.5-39.0

Tool 3 = #5 HSS Center Drill
Cutting Speed = 165-850
r/min = 1261-6494
in/tooth = .002-.006
in/min = 5.0-78.0

Tool 4 = .4219 inch (27/64) diameter HSS Drill
Cutting Speed = 165-850
r/min = 1494-7696
in/tooth = .002-.006
in/min = 6.0-92.0

Calculation required to add for the drill point on the .4219 inch diameter hole.

.211 * TAN 31° = .1268

1.125 + .1268 = 1.2518

Tool 5 = .4375 diameter HSS Reamer
Cutting Speed = 203
r/min = 1772
in/tooth = .003
in/min = 32.0

O0015
(CNC Machining Center Exercise #15)
(Date, By)
N10G90G20G80G40G49
(Tool #1 Face Mill 3.0 inch diameter 90° 5
  teeth Carbide)
N20T01M6
N30G54G0X3.725Y1.0
N40S1238M3
N50G43Z1.0H01
N60Z.2M08
N70G01Z0F10.0
N80X-3.725F216.0
N90Z.2
N100X3.725Y-1.0
N110Z0
N120X-3.725
N130Z.1
N140X3.5167Y0

N150Z-.1875F10.0
N160X1.7583Y-3.0455F216.0
N170X-1.7583
N180X-3.5167Y0
N190X-1.7583Y3.0455
N200X1.7583
N210X3.5167Y0
N220Z-.375F10.0
N230X1.7583Y-3.0455F216.0
N240X-1.7583
N250X-3.5167Y0
N260X-1.7583Y3.0455
N270X1.7583
N280X3.5167Y0
N290G80Z.1M09
N300G91G28Z0
N310M01
(Tool #2 1.0 inch diameter, HSS, 2 Flute
  End Mill)
(Cutter Diameter Compensation offset
  #D32)
N320T02M6
N330S1939M3
N340G90G20G80G40G49
N350G0G54X2.7Y.6
N360G43Z1.0H02
N370Z.1M08
N380G1Z-.375F10.0
N390X1.75Y0G41D32
N400X.875Y-1.5155F21.0
N410X-.875
N420X-1.75Y0
N430X-.875Y1.5155
N440X.875
N450X1.75Y0
N460G80G0Z.1M09
N470G91G28Z0
N480M01

(Tool #3 = #5 HSS Center Drill)
N490T03M6
N500S3878M03
N510G90G20G80G40G49
N520G0G54X.7071Y.7071
N530G43Z.1H03
N540G81Z-.25R.1F42.0
N550Y-.7071
N560X-.7071
N570Y.7071
N580G80Z.1M09
N590G91G28Z0
N600M01
(Tool 4 = .4219 27/64 diameter HSS Drill)
N610T04M6
N620S4595M03
N630G90G20G80G40G49
N640G0G54X.7071Y.7071
N650G43Z.1H04
N660G83Z-1.252Q.282R.1F49.0
N670Y-.7071
N680X-.7071
N690Y.7071
N700G80Z.1M09
N710G91G28Z0
N720M01
(Tool #5 = .4375 diameter HSS Reamer)
N730T05M6
N740S1772M03
N750G90G20G80G40G49
N760G0G54X.7071Y.7071
N770G43Z.1H05
N780G85Z-1.252R.1F32.0
N790Y-.7071
N800X-.7071
N810Y.7071
N820G80Z.1M09
N830G91G28Z0
N840G28X0Y0
N850M30

CNC Machining Center Subprogram Application

M98 and M99 and G68

CNC Machining Center Exercise #16 Program Code

Program to machine all of the holes and pocket for the drawing below. Subprogram application (M98 and M99) and G68 for coordinate system rotation for the slots.

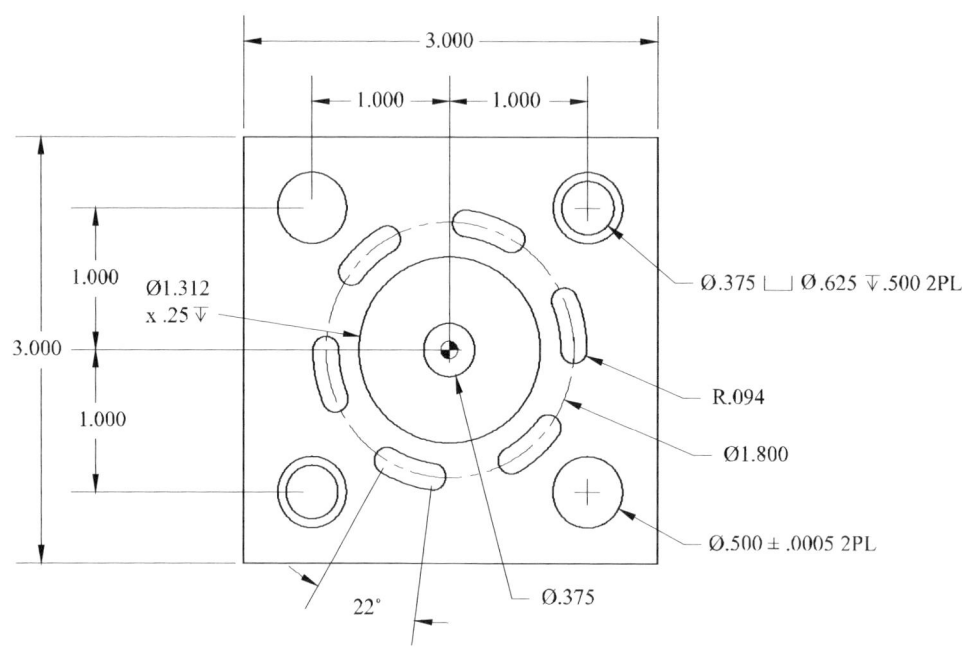

Figure 105 CNC Machining Center Programming Exercise 16

Tool 1 = .75 diameter 90° HSS Spot Drill
Cutting Speed = 165-850
r/min = 840-4329
in/tooth = .002-.006
in/min = 1.68-26.0

Tool 2 = 31/64 .4843 inch diameter HSS Drill
Cutting Speed = 165-850
r/min = 1301-6704
in/tooth = .002-.006
in/min = 5.2-80.4

Tool 3 = .375 inch diameter HSS Drill
Cutting Speed = 165-850
r/min = 1681-8658
in/tooth = .002-.006
in/min = 6.72-104.

Tool 4 = .3750 inch diameter HSS Reamer
Cutting Speed = 55
r/min = 560
in/tooth = .002
in/min = 6.7

Tool 5 = 5/8 inch diameter, HSS, 2 Flute End Mill
Cutting Speed = 165-850
r/min = 1008-5195
in/tooth = .002-.006
in/min = 4.0-62.3
Tool 6 = 1/8 inch diameter, HSS, 2 Flute End Mill
Cutting Speed = 165-850
r/min = 6000
in/tooth = .002
in/min = 24.0

Calculation required for the Spot Drill depth on the .5 diameter holes allowing .010 inch for burr removal.

.520/2 = .260 * TAN 45° = .260

Calculation required to add for the drill point on the 31/64 .4843 diameter hole.

.4843/2 = .2422 * TAN 31° = .1455

Calculation required to add for the drill point on the .375 diameter hole.

.375/2 = .1875 * TAN 31° = .113

O0016
(CNC Machining Center Exercise #16)
(Date, By)
N10G90G20G80G40G49
(Tool 1 = .75 diameter 90° HSS Spot Drill)

N20T01M6
N30G54G0X1.0Y1.0
N40S2585M3
N50G43Z1.0H01
N60Z.1M08
N70G99G81Z-.26R.1F10.3
N80X-1.0Y-1.0
N90Y1.0
N100X1.0Y-1.0
N110G80Z.1M09
N120G91G28Z0
N130M01
(Tool 2 = 31/64 .4843 inch diameter HSS Drill)
N140T02M6
N150G90G20G80G40G49
N160G54G0X-1.0Y1.0
N170S4003M3
N180G43Z1.0H02
N190Z.1M08
N200G99G83Z-.896R.1Q.323F32.
N210X1.0Y-1.0
N220G80Z.1M09
N230G91G28Z0
N240M01
(Tool 3 = .375 inch diameter HSS Drill)
N250T03M6
N260G90G20G80G40G49
N270G54G0X1.0Y1.0
N280S3489M3
N290G43Z1.0H03
N300Z.1M08
N310G99G83Z-.863R.1Q.25F28.
N320X-1.0Y-1.0
N330X0Y0
N340G80Z.1M09
N350G91G28Z0
N360M01
(Tool 4 = .3750 inch diameter HSS Reamer)
N370T03M6
N380G90G20G80G40G49
N390G54G0X-1.0Y1.0

N400S560M3
N410G43Z1.0H04
N420Z.1M08
N430G99G86Z-.875R.1F6.7
N440X1.0Y-1.0
N450G80Z.1M09
N460G91G28Z0
N470M01
(Tool 5 = 5/8 inch diameter, HSS, 2 Flute End Mill)
N480T05M6
N490G90G20G80G40G49
N500G54G0X1.0Y1.0
N510S3102M3
N520G43Z1.0H05
N530Z.1M08
N540G99G82Z-.5R.1P2.F24.8
N550X-1.0Y-1.0
N560G80Z.1
N570X.0082Y-.3334
N580G1Z-.25
N590X.0082
N600G3X.3335Y0.R.3335
N610G1X-.3335
N620G2X-.0082Y.3334R.3335
N630G1X.0082
N640G0Z.1
N650X.3435Y0
N660G1Z-.25
N670G3X0.Y.3435R.3435
N680X-.3435Y0.R.3435
N690X0.Y-.3435R.3435
N700X.3435Y0.R.3435
N710G0Z.1
N720G91G28Z0
N730M01
(Tool 6 = 1/8 inch diameter, HSS, 2 Flute End Mill)
N740T06M6
N750G90G20G80G40G49
N760G54G0X.931Y0
N770G68X0Y0R0.0
N780S6000M3

N790G43Z1.0H06
N800Z.1M08
N810G1Z-.25F24.
N820M98P3456
N830G0Z.1
N840G68X0Y0R60.0
N850G1Z-.25F6.16
N860M98P3456
N870G0Z.1
N880G68X0Y0R120.0
N890M98P3456
N900G0Z.1
N910G68X0Y0R180.0
N920M98P3456
N930G0Z.1
N940G68X0Y0R240.0
N950M98P3456
N960G0Z.1
N970G68X0Y0R300
N980M98P3456
N990G69
N1000G0Z.1M09
N1010G91G28Z0
N1020G28X0Y0A0
N1030M30

Subprogram for program #O0016

O3456
N1020G3X.8601Y.3563R.931
N1030X.8315Y.3754R.031
N1040X.8005Y.3444R.031
N1050X.8029Y.3326R.031
N1060G2X.869Y0.R.869
N1070G3X.9Y-.031R.031
N1080X.931Y0.R.031
N1090M99

CNC Machining Center Exercise #17 Program Code

Program to machine all of the holes and step cutouts in the block in the drawing below, using the G98 command with Canned Cycles.

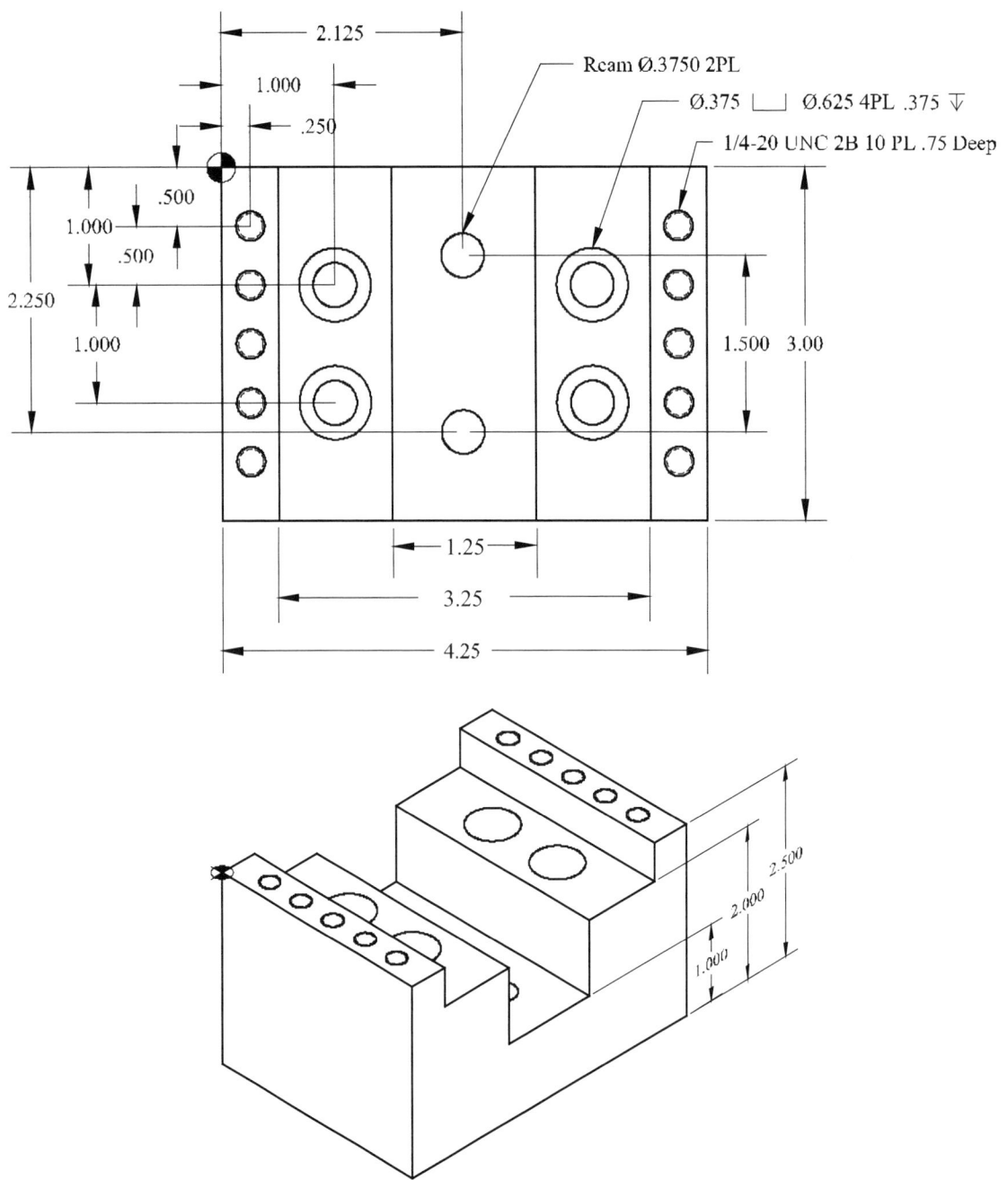

Figure 106 CNC Machining Center Programming Exercise 17

A 1.0 inch diameter 4 flute HSS End Mill could be used to rough out the steps leaving .03 inch for finish. In this answer program, the 3.0 inch Face Mill is chosen instead. This program is also a good candidate for the use of a subprogram for repetition of the hole locations.

Tool 1 = Face Mill, 3.0 inch diameter, 90°, 5 teeth, Carbide)
Cutting Speed = 90-685
r/min = 115-872
in/tooth = .020-.039
in/min = 12.0-170.0

Tool 2 = 1.0 inch diameter, HSS, 4 Flute Roughing End Mill
Cutting Speed = 25-140
r/min = 95-535
in/tooth = .001-.004
in/min = .380-8.6

Tool 3 = 1.0 inch diameter, HSS, 4 Flute End Mill
Cutting Speed = 25-140
r/min = 95-535
in/tooth = .001-.004
in/min = .380-8.6

Tool 4 = #5 HSS Center Drill
Cutting Speed = 25-140
r/min = 218-1222
in/tooth = .001-.004
in/min = .436-9.8

Tool 5 = #7 .201 inch diameter HSS Drill
Cutting Speed = 25-140
r/min = 475-2660
in/tooth = .001-.004
in/min = .950-21.0
Add a minimum of .200 inch depth to allow for the tap lead.

Tool 6 = 3/8 inch diameter HSS Drill
Cutting Speed = 25-140
r/min = 255-1426
in/tooth = .001-.004
in/min = .510-11.4

Tool 7 = 23/64 (.3594) inch diameter HSS Drill
Cutting Speed = 25-140
r/min = 266-1488
in/tooth = .001-.004
in/min = .532-11.9

Tool 8 = .3750 diameter HSS Reamer
Cutting Speed = 38
r/min = 387
in/tooth = .0025
in/min = 5.8

Tool 9 = 5/8 (.625) inch diameter, HSS, 4 Flute End Mill
Cutting Speed = 25-140
r/min = 153-856
in/tooth = .001-.004
in/min = .612-14.0

Tool 10 = 1/4 -20 Tap
Cutting Speed = 25
r/min = 382
in/tooth = .002
in/min = 19.0
382 * .05 = 19.0

O0017
(CNC Machining Center Exercise #17)
(Date, By)
N10G90G20G80G40G49
(Tool #1 Face Mill 3.0 inch diameter 90° 5 teeth Carbide)
N20T01M6
N30G54G0X2.125Y1.60
N40S494M3
N50G43Z1.0H01
N60Z.1M08
N70G01Z-.25F10.0
N80Y-4.6F18.0
N90G0Z.1
N100Y1.6

N110G01Z-.50F10.0
N120Y-4.6F18.0
N130G80Z.1M09
N140G91G28Z0
N150M01
(Tool 2 = 1.0 inch diameter, HSS, 4 Flute Roughing End Mill)
N160T02M6
N170G90G20G80G40G49
N180G54G0X2.125Y.60
N190S315M3
N200G43Z1.0H02
N210Z.1M08
N220G01Z-.75F20.0
N230Y-3.6F3.0
N240G0Z.1
N250Y.6
N260G01Z-1.5F20.0
N270Y-3.6F3.0
N280G80Z.1M09
N290G91G28Z0
N300M01
(Tool 3 = 1.0 inch diameter, HSS, 4 Flute End Mill)
(Cutter Diameter Compensation #D33)
N310T03M6
N320G90G20G80G40G49
N330G54G0X1.0Y.7
N340S315M3
N350G43Z1.0H03
N360Z.1M08
N370G01Z-.5F10.0
N380X.5Y.5G41D33
N390Y-4.0F3.0
N400X3.75F20.0
N410Y.5F3.0
N420G1Z-1.5F10.0
N430X1.5G41D33F20.0
N440Y-4.0F3.0
N450X2.75F20.0
N460Y.5F3.0

N470G80G40Z.1M09
N480G91G28Z0
N490M01
(Tool 4 = #5 HSS Center Drill)
N500T04M6
N510G90G20G80G40G49
N520G54G0X.25Y-.5
N530S720M3
N540G43Z1.0H04
N550Z.1M08
N560G81G99Z-.25R.1F3.6
N570Y-1.0
N580Y-1.5
N590Y-2.0
N600Y-2.5
N610X4.0
N620Y-2.0
N630Y-1.5
N640Y-1.0
N650Y-.5
N660G81G98X3.25Y-1.0Z-.75R-.4
N670Y-2.0
N680X1.0
N690Y-1.0
N700G81G98X2.125Y-.75Z-1.75R-1.4
N710Y-2.25
N720G80Z.1M09
N730G91G28Z0
N740M01
(Tool 5 = #7 .201 inch diameter HSS Drill)
N750T05M6
N760G90G20G80G40G49
N770G54G0X.25Y-.5
N780S1566M3
N790G43Z1.0H05
N800Z.1M08
N810G83G99Z-1.1Q.134R.1F7.8
N820Y-1.0
N830Y-1.5
N840Y-2.0
N850Y-2.5

N860X4.0
N870Y-2.0
N880Y-1.5
N890Y-1.0
N900Y-.5
N910G80Z.1M09
N920G91G28Z0
N930M01
(Tool 6 = 3/8 inch diameter HSS Drill)
N940T06M6
N950G90G20G80G40G49
N960G54G0X3.25Y-1.0
N970S841M3
N980G43Z1.0H06
N990Z.1M08
N1000G83G98Z-2.712Q.25R-.4F4.2
N1010Y-2.0
N1020X1.0
N1030Y-1.0
N1040G80Z.1M09
N1050G91G28Z0
N1060M01
(Tool 7 = 23/64 .3594 inch diameter HSS Drill)
N1070T07M6
N1080G90G20G80G40G49
N1090G54G0X2.125Y-.75
N1100S877M3
N1110G43Z1.0H07
N1120Z.1M08
N1130G83G99Z-2.608Q.24R-1.4F4.4
N1140Y-2.25
N1150G80Z.1M09
N1160G91G28Z0
N1170M01
(Tool 8 = .3750 diameter HSS Reamer)
N1180T08M6
N1190G90G20G80G40G49
N1200G54G0X2.125Y-.75
N1210S387M3
N1220G43Z1.0H08
N1230Z.1M08

N1240G85G99Z-2.75R-1.4F5.8
N1250Y-2.25
N1260G80Z.1M09
N1270G91G28Z0
N1280M01
(Tool 9 = 5/8 inch diameter, HSS, 4 Flute End Mill)
N1290T09M6
N1300G90G20G80G40G49
N1310G54G0X3.25Y-1.0
N1320S505M3
N1330G43Z1.0H06
N1340Z.1M08
N1350G82G98Z-.875R-.4P200F5.0
N1360Y-2.0
N1370X1.0
N1380Y-1.0
N1390G80Z.1M09
N1400G91G28Z0
N1410M01
(Tool 10 = ?-20 Tap)
N1420T010M6
N1430G90G20G80G40G49
N1440G54G0X.25Y-.5
N1450S382M3
N1460G43Z1.0H10
N1470Z.1M08
N1480G84G99Z-.75R.1F19.0
N1490Y-1.0
N1500Y-1.5
N1510Y-2.0
N1520Y-2.5
N1530X4.0
N1540Y-2.0
N1550Y-1.5
N1560Y-1.0
N1570Y-.5
N1580G80Z.1M09
N1590G91G28Z0
N1600G28X0Y0
N1610M30

CNC Machining Center Program Error Diagnosis Answers

Use the skills you have learned to identify the problems in the following program lines and program sections. You may refer to the text, "Programming of CNC Machines," Third Edition.

1. Use the CNC code to sketch a representation of the part being created by the following program.

O3001
N100G90G17G20G80G49
(3/8 2FL ENDMILL)
N105T1M6
N110G0G90G54X0.Y0.S1426M3
N108G43H1Z.1M8
N110G1Z-.1F6.33
N112G41D1Y6.
N114X1.Y7.
N116X1.5
N118X2.5Y6.
N120G3X4.5R1.
N122G1X11.Y2.5
N124Y1.
N126X10.Y0.
N128G40X0.
N130Z.1
N132M5
N134G91G0G28Z0.M9
N136G28X0.Y0.
N138M30

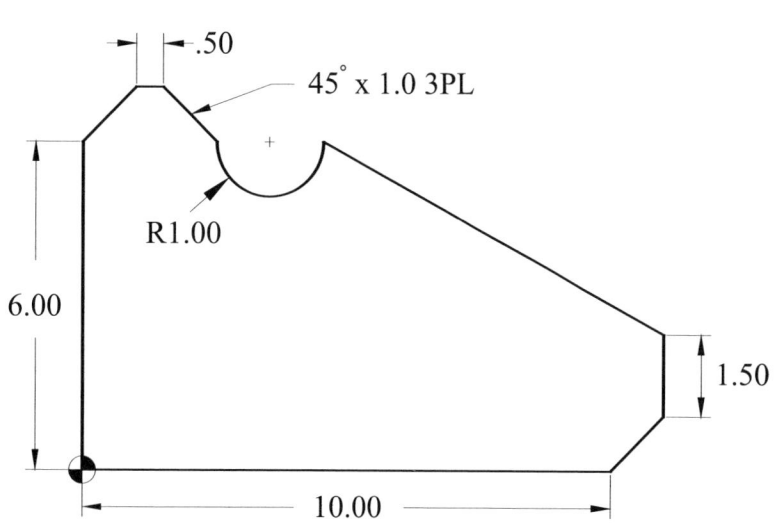

Figure 107
CNC Machining Center Error
Diagnosis Part Drawing

2. Identify the missing information in the following program line.

N250G02X-.375Y2.938

    Missing arc center locations or Radius (R) designation.

3. Identify the incorrect or missing information in the following program line.

N110X-4.625F12.

    Missing G01 with Feedrate

4. Identify the incorrect or missing information in the following program line.

N25S2500M4

    Incorrect Spindle direction code

5. Identify the missing information in the following program line.

N125G83G99Z-1.13R.1F3.6

    Missing pecking distance (Q value) in Canned Drilling Cycle

6. Identify the incorrect or missing information in the following program and/or subprogram.

O2010
N10G90G80G20G40G49M23
N15G00G54X-1.25Y.75S1000M03
N20G43Z1.0H01M08
N25G81G98Z-.35R.1F6.0
N30M98P7
N35G00G80X0
N40M21
N45G00X-1.25Y.75
N50G81G98Z-.35F6.R.1
N55M98P7
N60G00G80X0Y0
N65M23
N70M22
N75G00X-1.25Y.75
N80G81G98Z-.35F6.R.1

N85M98P7
N90G80G00X0Y0
N95M21
N100G00X-1.25Y.75
N105G81G98Z-.35F6.R.1
N110M98P7
N115G80Z1.0M09
N120M23
N125G91G28X0Y0Z0
N130M30

      Subprogram for Program 2010
O2011
N1X-2.5
N2X-3.75
N3Y1.5
N4X-2.5
N5X-1.25
N6Y2.25
N7X-2.5
N8X-3.75
N9M30

Improper program # call, for subprogram in line 30, 55, 85 and 110. The correct information should be N30M98P2011 in each line.
Improper subprogram ending in subprogram #2011. Line N9 should read N9M99.

7. Identify the incorrect or missing information in the following program line.

N310G01G41X-4.125Y0
      Missing cutter diameter compensation call (D#)

8. Identify the missing information in the following program line.

N10G90G20G80G49
      Missing cutter diameter compensation cancellation

9. Identify the missing information in the following program line.

N35G43Z1.0
      Missing tool height call (H number)

INDEX